T0366403

PORTFOLIO SOCIETY

Portfolio Society:
On the Capitalist Mode of Prediction

Ivan Ascher

ZONE BOOKS

near futures

© 2016 Ivan Ascher
ZONE BOOKS
633 Vanderbilt Street, Brooklyn, New York 11218

Printed in the United States of America.
Distributed by The MIT Press,
Cambridge, Massachusetts, and London, England.

Library of Congress Cataloging-in-Publication Data
Names: Ascher, Ivan, author
Title: Portfolio society: on the capitalist mode of prediction /
    Ivan Ascher.
Description: New York: Zone Books, [2016] | Includes
    bibliographical references and index.
Identifiers: LCCN 2016021176 | ISBN 9781935408741
    (hardcover: alk. paper)
Subjects: LCSH: Capital market. | Capitalism. | Securities. |
    Financial crises. | Marx, Karl, 1818–1883. Kapital.
Classification: LCC HG4523 .A775 2016 | DDC 335.4/12–DC23
LC record available at https://lccn.loc.gov/2016021176

CONTENTS

In memory of François and Bertrand

The Specter of Wall Street

A specter is haunting Europe—and much of the rest of the world, for that matter. Even the holy father, who back in the day had joined the czar, Metternich and Guizot, French Radicals, and German police spies in denouncing the evils of Communism, is now claiming that a "new tyranny" has come into existence—one that is "invisible and often virtual," but nonetheless successful in imposing "its own laws and rules" on all the rest of us.[1] The magazine *Rolling Stone*, meanwhile, is known around the world for its description of Goldman Sachs as a "a great vampire squid wrapped around the face of humanity," and Warren Buffett, the billionaire investor, is likewise celebrated for having described derivatives as "financial weapons of mass destruction."[2] As for the French socialist François Hollande, it was only once he resolutely declared "the world of finance" to be his "true adversary" that he succeeded in his quest for the presidency.[3] All in all, it would appear that the powers of old Europe and those of the New World have finally joined forces against a common enemy, forming a new Holy Alliance to exorcise this magical power that is the specter of Wall Street.[4]

Think about it: what financial crisis has not been blamed on the speculative excesses of Wall Street bankers or the arrogance of the overpaid "quants" among them? What austerity measures, what budget cuts, have not been justified by the demands of the bond markets or the credit rating agencies? And finally, what beleaguered Goldman

Sachs employee has not hurled back the accusations of greed onto the culture of his employer or that of Wall Street more generally?

Two things follow from this fact: first, that Wall Street is "already acknowledged to be itself a Power," as Karl Marx and Friedrich Engels might have put it, and a most frightening one at that; second, and no less importantly, that we must guard against simple denunciations of this genuinely terrifying power—lest we find ourselves disabled before this monster of unspeakable proportions and disciplined even further into submitting to its tyrannical dictates.[5] Indeed, it is high time that we meet our own "nursery tales" of the specter of Wall Street—if not with a manifesto of Wall Street itself (though that would be interesting), then with a proper critique of contemporary finance and the societies that live under its spell.

The present essay is my contribution to such a critique. It is a modest contribution, to be sure, and one that very much bears the stamp of its origins both in the so-called "subprime crisis" of 2007–2008 and in a certain Marxian tradition of critique. The narrative thus begins in January 2007, shortly before a wave of mortgage defaults among U.S. home owners brought about the collapse of the world's credit markets. It ends six and a half years later, with the much-publicized trial in New York City of a single Goldman Sachs employee charged with securities fraud. The analysis, meanwhile, proceeds through a creative appropriation of Karl Marx's *Capital*, volume 1—a seemingly sacred text of social theory that I interpret in a decidedly unorthodox way. My aim in this book, however, is neither to chronicle the financial crisis nor to present a new reading of Marx for its own sake.[6] It is, rather, to begin to theorize twin developments that Marx himself could not have anticipated, but that the crisis has helped reveal: the extraordinary rise of financial markets in recent decades and the concurrent development of what Gerald Davis has aptly called a "portfolio society," in which capitalist relations themselves have to a large extent become "securitized."[7]

As we will see, there is nothing new about financial markets or securitization per se. It has long been possible for investors to acquire shares in the ownership of a company, say, and for these shares to be treated as tradable assets ("securities") to be bought or sold on secondary markets. Likewise, it has been common practice throughout the history of capitalism for cash-strapped governments to issue sovereign bonds to which individuals—including foreign nationals—might then subscribe and which they might alienate in turn.[8] And finally, it has been possible since at least the eighteenth century for investors to bundle together claims to different income streams and to use them as "backing" for the issuance of new, tradable securities. This was done most recently (and most infamously) in the United States with subprime residential mortgages, but already in the 1770s, Swiss bankers were combining life annuities issued by the French state in order to issue safer securities of their own.[9] These are long-standing practices, in other words, that in and of themselves are almost unremarkable.

As we will also see, however, there is much about Anglo-American capitalism that has changed in recent decades, especially since the publication in 1952—by a young graduate student named Harry Markowitz—of the theory of "portfolio selection" to which this book owes its title.[10] Markowitz's argument, in retrospect, was a simple one: rational investors, he claimed, know very well that the future is uncertain and are therefore unlikely to bet all their money on the success of a single company, no matter how promising. Instead, they will tend to invest in a whole panoply of stocks and bonds, attuned as they are to the strategic importance of diversification. Rational investors do not and should not place all their eggs in one basket, in other words, and in selecting their investments, they should not merely consider expected returns; rather, they should attend to what each security contributes to their overall portfolio of assets—and this, in terms of risk as well as return.

A decade or so later, in 1964, it was another graduate student—William Sharpe—who helped turn this theory into practice by introducing a simple coefficient—he called it β—with which to determine a stock's sensitivity to the fluctuations of the overall market. A security with a β greater than 1 was one that would amplify market fluctuations; a security with a β lower than 1 would attenuate them.[11] With this coefficient, Sharpe reasoned, investors could follow Markowitz's advice without having to determine how each potential investment covaried with every other asset in their portfolio. They needed only to consider how the price of a given security moves in relation to the market as a whole and thus construct a properly diversified portfolio that would match their desired level of risk and return.

Though these analyses may have seemed at first like the purely academic musings of precocious graduate students, the principles they outlined—the principles of modern portfolio theory—were quickly internalized by theorists and practitioners alike at a time when markets in general were undergoing significant transformation. Starting in the 1970s, indeed, other intellectual and technological advances—coupled with the demise of the international monetary system that had been established at Bretton Woods in 1944—set the stage for a dramatic expansion in the use of options, futures, and other so-called "derivative contracts."[12] These are contracts that allow investors not only to manage the various new risks associated with globalization (such as exchange rate risk, country risk, and so on), but also to construct and continuously maintain carefully calibrated portfolios that would—in principle—correspond to their chosen levels of risk exposure. As we will see, the development and widespread adoption of the Black-Scholes-Merton model for options pricing succeeded in giving investors the confidence that they could continuously and scientifically hedge what would otherwise have been untenable positions simply by combining the continuous buying and selling of stocks and bonds with the concurrent buying and selling of options and other derivatives. More and more capital flowed to financial markets as a result, and investors—these were institutional investors, increasingly—could now engage in a strategy of incessant trading that allowed them to regulate their risk exposure while simultaneously providing the market with all the liquidity it needed to be plausibly considered efficient, as per the strictures of the newly dominant paradigm.[13]

In sum, by the time Markowitz and Sharpe were finally recognized by the Nobel committee in 1990 for "their pioneering work in the theory of financial economics," the world of global finance had indeed been refashioned along the lines that they had sketched.[14] It was now possible to speak meaningfully of a market portfolio, as per Sharpe's formulation, and risk itself had become a thing that could be quantified and readily exchanged.[15] And by the winter of 2007–2008—the winter of our discontent, when the most recent crisis came into view—it was the entire fabric of society that had been transformed: a third of all profits in the United States were occurring in the financial sector, levels of public and private debt had reached record highs, and access to financial markets—once the privilege of an elite few—had officially become democratized.[16] Commercial banks could now invest with abandon in the world's financial markets (the Glass-Steagall Act of 1933 having just been repealed), an ever greater share of people's retirement savings were being managed by a handful of pension funds (their future, therefore, placed at the mercy of the market's fluctuations), and the U.S. government itself was actively fostering an "ownership society" in which everyone from Wall Street to Main Street would have some skin in the game.[17] Some people were managing billion-dollar hedge funds, while others were merely placing their savings in a retirement account; some were using their home as collateral for a second mortgage, while others were borrowing heavily on behalf of their fellow citizens; but all of them, somehow, were playing the market. Or more precisely, as they would soon find out, some were playing, while others were being played.

The fact of this transformation—the fact, that is, that financial markets now appear as a force of their own while simultaneously mediating an increasing range of social relations—is incontrovertible. But what is the significance of this transformation, one wonders, for our understanding of capitalist relations themselves? More specifically, what are the implications of this transformation for a critique of political economy of the kind inaugurated by Marx a century and a half ago? Marx himself, after all, may have taught us to expect—if not to accept—that the production of goods in capitalist societies would be organized around monetized trade and the pursuit of profit, but what should we make of the fact that even our *promises* are now being made only to be "sold" or otherwise exchanged, as if the mere buying and selling of financial assets were sufficient to turn an uncertain future into a source of security in the present? It seems clear that the very frailty of our social relations—the possibility, say, that we might falter in our commitments to one another—can now be measured and speculated on, but what does it mean to live in a world where *risk itself* can be treated as something to be bought or sold, and is this not to some extent comparable to the ways that labor was once thought of in the European nineteenth century?

Likewise, many readers of Marx have argued over the years that the "free market" is but a liberal fiction—one that allows for workers to be exploited while their employers are free to set the terms of the wage contract. But what is the pertinence of such an insight when in so many places it is the credit relation, rather than the wage, that now appears as the main site of profit-making and political struggle? What are the narratives legitimating these new power relations, and what new forms of violence might we be committing (or suffering) in their name? And finally, even if we assume that some people have always benefitted from the vulnerability of others, whether by speculating on the possible misfortunes in their future or simply by paying them a pittance in exchange for their labor, when and how did such speculation become not only generalized, but seemingly required in order for anyone to imagine a future in the first place? Surely we can concede to Adam Smith that dividing labor has increased its productivity, just as we may concede that the advent of securitization has increased liquidity in financial markets, allowing investors to borrow more capital and thus to multiply the potential return on their investments. But at what cost is such "leverage"—as it is so aptly named—ever achieved, and on whose shoulders exactly? After all, if Archimedes was surely right to imagine that he could move the earth, did he not also acknowledge that he would need a place on which to stand?[18] Who bears the burden of financialization, one wonders, and whose world does it truly lift?

In 1867, some twenty years after the *Manifesto*, Marx prefaced his own critique of political economy with the observation that "beginnings are always difficult in all sciences."[19] And yet, as is well known, Marx nonetheless found a starting point in the study of commodities in exchange—on the assumption, as he put it, that for "bourgeois society" (or "civil society," as it might also be called [*bürgerliche Gesellschaft*]), "the commodity-form of the product of labour or the value-form of the commodity [was] the economic cell form."[20] In light of all that precedes, I propose in the following to proceed from a different starting point, on the assumption that the "economic cell form" of our own portfolio society is no longer the "commodity-form of the product of labour," as in Marx's formulation, but the security form of capital itself.[21]

CHAPTER ONE

Capitalism: A Horror Story

> —We're sorry. It's not us. It's the monster. The bank isn't like a man.
> —Yes, but the bank is only made of men.
> —No, you're wrong there—quite wrong there. The bank is something else than men. It happens that every man in a bank hates what the bank does, and yet the bank does it. The bank is something more than men, I tell you. It's the monster. Men made it, but they can't control it. (John Steinbeck, *The Grapes of Wrath*)

Late one evening in January 2007, on the twenty-sixth floor of Goldman Sachs's headquarters in lower Manhattan, a Frenchman by the name of Fabrice Tourre set out to write an e-mail to his girlfriend back in London, Marine Serres. The young banker—he was only twenty-eight at the time—was a graduate of the prestigious École Centrale in Paris, but had moved to take a much-coveted job at Goldman Sachs in the early 2000s. (In another e-mail to another girlfriend a few days later, Tourre would complain—or boast—that after only six years, he was already considered a "dinosaur" in the business and was expected to serve as a mentor to younger colleagues.[1]) Like many other French bankers working on Wall Street, Tourre was known as a "quant"—that is, an expert in quantitative finance, and had been recruited for his mathematical talents more than for his business savvy or social skills.[2]

More specifically, Tourre's expertise was in the area of structured finance—meaning, in his case, that he was responsible for "structuring" and marketing what were known as synthetic collateralized debt obligations (CDOs)—speculative contracts linked to the performance of subprime residential mortgages.

For several years—roughly since the time Tourre had begun working at Goldman Sachs—the market for synthetic CDOs had grown at a rapid pace. A boom in the American real estate market, coupled with the development of new risk-management techniques and significant changes in the regulatory framework governing the use of so-called "derivative" contracts, had made it possible for lenders to extend residential mortgages (albeit expensive ones) to individuals whose credit history had once branded them as too risky.[3] These subprime loans, as they were called, were then pooled together and sold to investors as duly rated slices or "tranches" (a process known as securitization), which were then pooled together with other tranches and securitized anew. Other investors, meanwhile—with the help of individuals such as Tourre—could then enter into the type of synthetic CDOs just described or the credit default swaps (CDSs) of which they were composed—insurance contracts, of a sort, which allowed them in effect to speculate on the likelihood that subprime borrowers would make good on their mortgage payments.

The system worked. So long as houses kept appreciating and lenders kept finding investors on whom to offload the loans and the risks they carried, it was a win-win situation: home ownership rates grew to unprecedented levels (reaching an all-time high of 69 percent in 2005), giving credence to the government's talk of a new ownership society, and the profits derived from financing these mortgages increased accordingly.[4] Starting in 2006, however, "something ominous began to happen in the United States" as the number of foreclosures in cities such as Cleveland and Detroit suddenly started to rise.[5] By January 2007, over 14 percent of all subprime mortgages in the United States had been delinquent for sixty days.[6] This was a bad sign for the subprime borrowers, to be sure, but it was a bad sign also for all those—and there were many—who had bought exposure to the risks of default associated with such loans. Even the *Financial Times* struck a note of concern when on January 19 it cited various sources (some of them anonymous) describing what they perceived as an unprecedented level of risk exposure in the market. As one of the sources put it, "I don't think there has ever been a time in history when such a large portion of the riskiest credit assets have been owned by such financially weak institutions…with very limited capacity to withstand adverse credit events and market downturns."[7] As for the author of the article, Gillian Tett, she herself evoked the unnerving emergence of a "brave new financial world" and a growing sense of "unease" that was bubbling within it.[8]

The *Financial Times*'s analysis evidently resonated with Tourre, who forwarded the story to Serres with the following recommendation: "Darling you should take a look at this article…. Very insightful…. More and more leverage in the system, the entire structure could collapse at any moment." In an awkward mix of French and English, Tourre went on in a jargon that he knew she would understand (she, too, was a French expatriate, working for Goldman in its London office): "*Seul survivant potentiel* [Only potential survivor], the fabulous Fab (as Mitch would kindly call me, even though there is nothing fabulous abt me, just kindness, altruism and deep love for some gorgeous and super-smart French girl in London), standing in the middle of all these complex, highly leveraged, exotic trades he created without necessarily understanding all the implications of those monstruosities [*sic*]!!!"[9]

A couple of months passed, but Tourre's concerns did not subside. In an e-mail dated March 7, he told Serres that things were "not looking good for the U.S. subprime business." "According to Sparks [Tourre's superior at Goldman]," he explained, "that business is totally dead, and the poor little subprime borrowers aren't going to live long!!!"[10] Tourre himself expected to be fine, though; he had even devised an exit strategy and would leave the subprime sector before "the beginning of distressed trading."[11] In fact, he was already at work looking for a new position in London, where, at long last, he and Serres could be reunited.

The rest, as they say, is history. In the weeks and months that followed, Tourre's premonition proved correct—for the most part. Subprime borrowers kept defaulting in ever greater numbers—in excess of what the banks' models expected, and the "unease" that Gillian Tett had described rapidly turned to panic. As the wave of foreclosures continued to swell, engulfing middle-class neighborhoods in Florida, California, Arizona, and Nevada, the "distressed trading" predicted by Tourre began in earnest. Bear Stearns was saved, at the demand of the federal government, but Lehman Brothers was let go; it filed for bankruptcy protection on September 15, 2008, causing the world's credit markets to seize up. With countless other banks, corporations, and even national governments on the brink of collapse, the U.S. Congress on October 3 had to agree to a $700 billion bailout, which did succeed in stemming the tide, but by the spring of 2009, an estimated $50 trillion in asset values had already been destroyed worldwide, and an untold number of people had been laid off from their jobs, displaced from their homes, or both.[12]

———————

If there is a silver lining to the financial crisis of 2008 that Fabrice Tourre so uncannily predicted, it may be simply that for the first time since the Great Depression, described by John Steinbeck in *The Grapes of Wrath*, many of us in the Global North have finally become aware of the extraordinary—and terrifying—power of financial institutions, or what is often referred to simply as "Wall Street." We had long known, of course, that finance is a crucial component of any market society, necessary for the production of wealth (or the exploitation of workers, depending on your point of view), and we may even have had an inkling of the growing importance of financial markets. But for many people on the Left, especially, finance remained something of a background condition—something one might find in the business section of the *Times*, say, or somewhere deep in the third volume of *Capital*. We each had our credit cards and our credit card bills, and some of us even had mortgages, but these all seemed like very personal matters. And since most of us were not running corporations or presidential campaigns, we could mostly afford to ignore what Bill Clinton could not—namely, that the world was increasingly at the mercy of "the Federal Reserve and a bunch of fucking bond traders."[13]

But then it hit us. When the struggles of middle-class home owners in Florida or Arizona, through an extraordinarily rapid succession of events, resulted in the collapse of some of the country's most reputable banks, and indeed, of entire economies halfway around the world; when financial techniques that had been originally devised to diffuse and distribute risk turned out only to amplify an already global crisis; and when the resulting threat of economic collapse prompted political leaders of all stripes to rally behind massive government bailouts of banks and other financial institutions (all the while leaving ordinary borrowers to fend for themselves in the face of foreclosure), we began to realize how globalized and integrated financial markets had become, how financialized our everyday lives really were, and how beholden to the financial industry our governments and central banks were likely to remain.

In the years since the so-called "subprime crisis" of 2008, thankfully, many analyses have already been proposed that help us make sense both of the crisis itself and of the disturbing trends it revealed.[14] There are those, as I have already suggested, for whom what the subprime crisis revealed was mostly the hubris of modern financiers—

mathematical wizards such as Fabrice Tourre, who, thinking they had contained or even eliminated risk, had in fact rendered it "systemic," releasing it unto the world like a force that they could no longer control.[15]

There are those, meanwhile, for whom the crisis of 2008 and the horrors it revealed were both the result and a symptom of society having lost sight of the true mission of finance, which is, presumably, to aid in the production of "real wealth."[16] On this view, the derivatives themselves may not have been to blame, but the success of these techniques—coupled with a fair bit of governmental deregulation and a resulting increase in the amount of proprietary trading—turned even the most staid and respectable of investment banks into reckless and rapacious speculators, zombielike institutions that were not only able to live on despite their "toxic assets," but were able as a result to threaten the entire financial system from within.[17]

There are those, finally, who have insisted that the crisis be recognized for what it is: a crisis in capitalism—perhaps even a crisis *of* capitalism—of the kind first theorized by Marx more than a century and a half ago. On this view, while the current "global slump" may find its proximate causes in the greedy machinations of financial engineers, the rise of finance itself can be understood only in light of the larger dynamics of capitalist accumulation.[18] According to Robert Brenner, for instance, it is the "steadily declining vitality of the advanced capitalist economies over three decades" that explains the rise in public and private borrowing since 1973 and is thus the "fundamental source of today's crisis."[19] For David Harvey, likewise, it is the fact that capital "cannot abide limits" that accounts for both the extraordinary expansion of the financial sector since the 1980s and its no less extraordinary difficulties in 2008. Capital is not a "thing" but a "process," as Harvey points out, and it is "fundamentally about putting money into circulation to make more money."[20] Thus when, in the 1970s, the relative strength of labor in the capitalist core came to be seen as an impediment to growth, it was seen as necessary to dismantle organized labor and outsource jobs to the periphery. And when it turned out, not long thereafter, that the newly disempowered working class was no longer able to purchase the goods it was producing, capital was once again confronted with a limit that it had somehow to circumvent. It was at this point that cheap credit was made available, allowing the circulation process to resume, but inevitably setting the stage for a momentous crisis down the road.

Others, of course, have been more willing to depart from the Marxist *doxa* and to describe financialization and the accompanying rise of neoliberalism as themselves marking "a new phase in the evolution of capitalism."[21] But even in such accounts, it is understood that while the rise of financialization may be without precedent, it is not without explanation. And that while there is much that is terrifying about contemporary Wall Street—be it the "monstruosities" evoked by Tourre, the "great vampire squid" described by *Rolling Stone*, or the "zombie banks" so roundly denounced by countless others—it should neither be explained away by some tale of scientists gone mad nor reduced to some anomalous departure from what a true market economy should look like. If anything, it is probably best to recognize Wall Street's monstrosity as but a normal feature of capitalism and as very much in keeping with the horrors that Marx himself described when he so vividly remarked that capital is "vampire-like" and "dripping from head to toe, from every pore, with blood and dirt."[22]

The analysis offered in the following pages, as will soon become apparent, is in many ways akin to the ones just evoked. Like Brenner, Harvey, and countless others, I turn to the writings of Karl Marx—and more specifically, to the first volume of *Capital*—in an attempt to develop a critique of contemporary finance and its increasing importance in Anglo-American society. Like them, I understand the rise of financial markets and financialization as part of a larger story of capitalism's historical development. And like them, finally, I do not paint the capitalist in "rosy colours" any more than Marx did; indeed, in many ways, the story I propose may be read as but another "nursery tale" about the specter of Wall Street—one that should be taken with more than a single grain of salt.[23]

But where others have turned to Marx chiefly in order to explain the newly ascendant character of finance or to relate the process of financialization to attributes and tendencies of the capitalist mode of production (which are often presumed to be already known), I turn to Marx's text with a slightly different set of questions and concerns. More than an explanation of financial capital or its rise, indeed, and more (or less) than a properly "Marxist" analysis of contemporary finance, what I propose is something of a thought experiment. Specifically, I wonder: What if the developments just evoked were to be seen not only as the latest chapter in the history of the capitalist mode of production, but as a defining feature of a new and distinctly uncanny mode of *prediction* and *protection*? What if ours were not simply to be thought of as a "civil society" (*bürgerliche Gesellschaft*) mediated by monetized exchange, but as a historically unique *portfolio society* in which capital's relation to its own future (and hence everyone's relation to the future) is itself mediated by financial markets?

After all, while Marx was surely right to emphasize that "man" is a producing animal and that he may in this regard be unique among all species, is it not likewise the case that man is also uniquely prone to worrying about the future? Or, at the very least, is it not the case that when producing what he thinks he will need to survive, man tends both to imagine or predict possible futures and to protect himself accordingly, in ways that are both distinctly human and historically specific?[24]

Let me put it differently. When Marx in 1867 declared that the "worst architect" compares favorably to "the best of bees" in that he first "raises his structure in imagination before he erects it in reality," it was evidently still possible for him to imagine the architect as a kind of demiurge working alone, just as it was apparently possible for many of his readers to think of the production process as somehow separate from the mode of its financing.[25] In today's global cities, however, it is not only self-evident that the building of an office tower, say,

> A spider conducts operations which resemble those of a weaver, and a bee would put many a human architect to shame by the construction of her honeycomb cells. But what distinguishes the worst architect from the best of bees is that the architect builds the cell in his mind before he constructs it in wax. At the end of every labour process, a result emerges which had already existed ideally. Man not only effects a change of form in the materials of nature; he also realizes his own purpose in those materials. And this is a purpose he is conscious of, it determines the mode of his activity with the rigidity of a law, and he must subordinate his will to it. (Marx, *Capital*, vol. 1, p. 284)

will require the energies and collaboration of countless individuals; it is also apparent that any such project will be both heavily mediated by finance and shot through with calculations regarding the various risks and costs attendant to construction. Indeed, it is quite possible that a property developer in London or Singapore, anticipating a rise in the demand for real estate, might decide to prerent office space in a structure it has yet to build, only to use these commitments by its future tenants to issue commercial mortgage-backed securities. The so-called "completion risk" would thus be shifted onto the tenants (themselves well-respected players in the world of investment banking), but this in turn is what would allow the project to begin in the first place.[26] As for the engineering firm that has been tasked with construction proper, it, too, might wish to manage its specific risks with some financial engineering of its own—by entering into forward contracts with its suppliers, say (thereby guaranteeing delivery of materials at a date and price set in advance), or by acquiring "weather derivatives" to hedge the risk of unwanted weather events (as might also be done by the owner of a vineyard or a ski resort). Even the *best* of architects is liable to fail, after all, and for this reason alone, she would be well advised to enter into all the appropriate insurance contracts.[27]

The point of this digression is simply this: while Marx's analysis in *Capital* certainly remains a helpful guide, even in a capitalist landscape radically transformed by finance, our own analysis must proceed from a different starting point. As I have already suggested, the "economic cell form" of our own societies appears no longer to be the "commodity-form of the product of labour," as in Marx's formulation, but the financial derivative, the futures contract, or better yet, the security form of capital itself. After all, does it not appear that risk, rather than labor, is now considered the fount of value—or at the very least, the central category of concern for those dealing in the buying and selling of financial securities?

Marx, in his own day, exposed the various ways that society's commitment to "growth" (as we would now call it) not only depends on the commodification of human labor or labor power, but ultimately results in the creation of an immiserated proletariat—a population of individuals whose lives are almost entirely reduced to their sole capacity to labor. But could it not be said that our own societies' obsessive quest for ever-greater security, economic or otherwise (after all, the so-called "securitization" of mortgages is not an isolated phenomenon), is similarly related to our increasing preoccupation with measuring probabilities or assessing people's creditworthiness? And could this not account—at least in part—for the chronic *in*security that is so widely felt?[28] Indeed, could it not be said that increasing precarity, more than mere immiseration, is now the better descriptor for today's proletarian condition?

The language of class, it is true, has fallen out of favor in much of the capitalist core, but this does not necessarily mean that class divisions no longer exist. It could simply be that the terms of the divisions have changed and that the struggle—"now hidden, now open"—is no longer between "freeman and slave, patrician and plebeian, lord and serf, guild-master and journeyman" or even between capitalist and worker, but between the investor, invariably "sophisticated," and the always already "subprime" borrower.[29] What would it mean, then (with apologies to Marx and Thomas Piketty) to write *Capital* in the twenty-first century?[30] Or what would it mean, at any rate, to begin a critique of contemporary social relations in the language not of the nineteenth, but of the twenty-first century—a century that is obsessed not with production, labor, or vampires, but with prediction, risk, and (why not?) zombies? We know already that the vampire squid is less of a real squid than it is an octopus; we know also that the zombie, while similar to the vampire, is not quite the same as the latter.[31] But what *is* the distinctive logic of today's zombie capitalism?[32] How does it live? And more importantly, how does it die?

The analysis I propose, as the reader will have guessed, is shamelessly derivative. While its animating concerns are resolutely contemporary, the basic structure of the argument is provided entirely by (a certain reading of) the nineteenth-century text that is Karl Marx's *Capital*, volume I. Marx's analysis in this work, we will see, proceeds both within and against the categories of the day: *Capital*, as per its subtitle, is indeed *A Critique of Political Economy*, which is why it begins where bourgeois political economy also begins: in the realm of exchange. My own analysis in Chapter 2 ("A Monstrous Collection of Securities") thus begins similarly in today's financial markets, where financial securities, like the commodities of yore, are both objects of use and the "material bearers of exchange value"[33]—or more precisely, *hedging* value. What is it, I ask, that these financial contracts have in common and that allows them to be hedged for one another? And what, if anything, is expressed in this incessant process of hedging and exchange? According to Marx, at least, it was the generalized exchange of commodities that allows for the expression as value of human labor in general. Could it not be said that in contemporary financial markets, the generalized hedging of financial securities for one another is likewise what allows for the expression of market risk as volatility and hence, perhaps, as a certain form of value?

These are awkward questions, and the analysis in Chapter 2—modeled as it is on Marx's already improbable analysis of the commodity—makes for a somewhat arduous beginning. The chapter may be especially trying for French readers, who—according to Marx—are notoriously impatient and eager "to know the connection between general principles and the immediate questions that have aroused their passions."[34] If those readers wish to skip ahead, they have my blessing. They should simply know that where Marx speaks of a "fetishism" that attaches to products of labor wherever they are produced as commodities—that is, wherever they are produced for exchange by alienated workers laboring in isolation from one another—I claim that we find a similar fetishism in today's financial markets.[35] These are markets that allow us to take risks together, undoubtedly, but where the distinctly social character of our risk-taking relations appears to us in a most curious form—as relations among the securities themselves. And much as the commodities we covet do not readily admit of their humble origins in relations of production, financial securities likewise tend to conceal the speculative relations on which they depend, but which they also mediate.

Whether this fetishism will ever disappear, who knows? But in the meantime, we must consider both what it makes feasible and what it conceals. In the nineteenth century, Marx wondered how it was possible for the mere exchange of commodities to generate so much wealth for some and so much misery for the others. He found the answer by following a figure he called "Moneybags" (*Geldbesitzer*) to the market and seeing what he found.[36] Today, a similar question haunts our discussions of financial markets: How is it possible, indeed, for the incessant trade of financial securities to generate increasing economic security for the financier while creating ever greater vulnerability for the rest of us? Taking another leaf out of Marx's playbook, Chapter 3 ("Finding Safety in Numbers") follows Moneybags to the market once again and examines what he encounters. In the nineteenth century, as we will see, what Moneybags found was a unique commodity, labor power, the use value of which possessed "the peculiar property of being a source of value."[37] More accurately, what he found were individuals who had property in their own person and were thus free to alienate their labor power in exchange for a wage. They did not have much else to their name, of course, which gave Moneybags the upper hand: he could pay them just enough to reproduce their labor power, and they would produce more value in return. Today, Moneybags seems to have gotten lucky once again: the people he finds are free not only to sell their labor power, but also to take out a loan, alienating their credibility along the way. This, we will see, not only means that lenders can provide money and collect interest. It also means, remarkably, that lenders themselves can borrow more, the more they lend—as if control over the means of *prediction* were what allowed them to turn other people's weakness into the source of their own strength.

How did this all come to pass? Chapter 4 ("From Vagabond to Subprime") offers one possible answer to this question. Like Marx's final chapters in *Capital*, on the "so-called primitive accumulation," this penultimate chapter tells a story of how a certain commons was enclosed and how new social relations have developed as a result. Since the 1970s, the collapse of the Bretton Woods system, the dismantling of the welfare state, and the concurrent rise of financial markets have not only exposed the populations of entire countries to new levels of uncertainty, they have also forced them to seek protection wherever they can while simultaneously exposing them to new forms of risk. Much as the English peasants of the Tudor era were forced by the enclosure movement to leave the countryside for neighboring towns, their descendants since the Thatcher years have had to seek refuge in the City of London or in other financial districts around the world, where, as they now find, they are being refashioned by new forms of power and discipline. In the fifth and final chapter ("When Goldman Broke the Law"), at long last, the narrative strays from that of *Capital* and returns instead to New York City, where perhaps we will find some closure on this crisis of ours. Or perhaps not.

CHAPTER TWO

A Monstrous Collection of Securities

The Museum of American Finance, at the intersection of William Street and Wall Street in New York City, boasts an impressive collection of financial securities, including thousands of stocks and bonds dating all the way from the eighteenth century to the present. Among the highlights of the collection, according to the museum's catalog, are a "1792 U.S. Treasury bond issued to George Washington bearing one of the first known uses of the dollar sign, a $100,000 bond issued to Andrew Carnegie in 1901," as well as "an 1869 Erie Railway certificate signed by Jay Gould."[1] One of my personal favorites is a so-called "Disney" bond, of the kind that was issued in the 1940s by the U.S. Treasury War Finance Committee, beautifully illustrated with several Walt Disney characters—evidently in the hope that parents both loving and patriotic would buy war bonds for their children.

Behind each of these artifacts, as the museum's descriptions make poignantly clear, there lies a story—in many cases, an important one in the context of American history. Thus, the $100,000 bond issued to Carnegie, for instance, is a trace of a notable transaction, one that involved John Pierpont Morgan, famed banker and financial deal maker, and Carnegie—who by then was close to retirement after a distinguished career as an entrepreneur. The deal—the acquisition by J. P. Morgan of the Carnegie Steel Company and its transformation into the United States Steel Corporation—would mark the culmination of

Carnegie's rags-to-riches story and assure J. P. Morgan's place in the pantheon of American finance as the person responsible for the largest industrial takeover in U.S. history to date.

For all of their value as historical curiosities, however, and despite the famous signatures or cartoon characters that might adorn them, the various bonds on display at the museum remain, fundamentally, quite simple objects. They are merely contracts, written documents that bind their signatories to certain commitments and promises while at the same time also binding them to each other, as each of the parties involved comes to depend on the other in their respective (or shared) pursuits. Thus, Carnegie and Morgan, in the case at hand, may be said to have benefited from the issuance of this bond—as did, arguably, the world of American philanthropy, which Carnegie did much to shape. And needless to say, the U.S. war effort benefited greatly from the patriotic support of countless American parents, whose children in turn received the assurance of a steady income and a purportedly free world in which to spend it.

When we consider them as pieces of paper under a glass case in a museum, then, financial securities confront us as ordinary and worldly things ("extremely obvious" and "trivial" things, as Marx once said of the commodity), contracts of the kind that have been drafted for millennia and that have been traded for centuries—at least since the opening of the Amsterdam Stock Exchange in 1602.[2] But if we transport ourselves only a block and a half west, from the Museum of American Finance to the New York Stock Exchange, or travel three miles toward the Midtown Tunnel to the corporate offices of JPMorgan Chase, the scene we encounter is altogether different.[3] There, instead of paper bonds in glass display cases, we see three-letter ticker symbols and color-coded numbers flashing across computer screens; instead of aging docents recounting the early days of the American railroad, young men in front of their Bloomberg terminals hustling to make a trade. It is as if the Disney characters had somehow leapt off the page and onto the screen and were now frantically dancing to the music of *Fantasia*.[4]

On some level, there is nothing particularly new about this: for many years the NYSE has been the site of financial transactions and trades, as have investment banks such as Goldman Sachs or J. P. Morgan. And yet something has decidedly changed in recent decades, both on the trading floors of Wall Street and in the society that surrounds them. Starting in the 1970s, already, the size of financial markets started to grow as new securities were being devised and an ever-increasing number of trades were being carried out. By now, however, it is not only the size of financial markets that is different. It is the very nature and "spirit" of financial exchange that have changed. Simply put, where financial markets were once thought to be in the service of those—be they individuals, corporations, or sovereign nations—that needed capital, it is now the markets themselves that appear to be calling the shots, not only setting the terms under which production is undertaken, but more generally yet, setting the terms under which companies, governments, and even households are now able to envisage the future and act in the present.

It is not the first time, mind you, that the world has seen such a peculiar transformation. In the nineteenth century, Marx described societies of a new type—"societies where the capitalist mode of production prevailed," as he called them—where the pursuit of value had

> The wealth of societies in which the capitalist mode of production prevails appears as an 'immense collection of commodities'; the individual commodity appears as its elementary form. Our investigation therefore begins with the analysis of the commodity. (Marx, *Capital*, vol. 1, p. 125)

become an end in itself and where the production of surplus value, therefore, had in turn become something of an organizing principle.[5]

Man's productive activity in these societies was no longer dictated by the arbitrary whim of the landlord or monarch (as it arguably once was), nor was it organized according to what goods people might need (as Marx thought it should be), but by how much money these goods might fetch *in exchange.* In fact, these were societies where the commodity form had become so generalized that even the production process—the process whereby society produced the things it needed—was itself mediated by monetized exchange. People had to sell their own labor power in order to make the things they needed, in other words, and they had to go to the market in order merely to acquire the things they had made. As in all societies, it was still the collective labor of all producers that created the nation's wealth, but that was not how things presented themselves. Instead, the distinctly social character of relations of production appeared to the producers in a mystified form, as relations between the products themselves. Or as Marx put in a passage already quoted, "the wealth of societies in which the capitalist mode of production prevails appears as an 'immense collection of commodities' [*eine 'ungeheure Warensammlung'*]; the individual commodity appears as its elementary form. Our investigation therefore begins with the analysis of the commodity."[6]

Marx himself made much of the difficulty of his opening chapter in *Capital* and of the originality of the argument therein—and with good reason. Any schoolboy at the time, I suppose, would have recognized that iron had to be mined or that wheat had to be planted and harvested before these products could be brought to market, and it had long been shown by David Ricardo, Adam Smith, and others that labor is the source of value, but it was Marx who most clearly pointed out that it is the labor of *all* of society that is at issue and that it is the amount of "socially necessary labour time" that determines the magnitude of a commodity's value, not the amount of time actually expended by any one particular miner or farmer in the production of any one commodity.[7] And it was Marx, also, who best described what he called the "fetishism" that attaches to products of labor when they are produced as commodities—a fetishism that allows the expression of value in exchange while at the same time concealing its origins in the realm of production.

But what is the relevance of Marx's analysis, one wonders, when the very phenomenology of capital seems to have changed? Are we to believe that labor is no longer the source of value, merely because the wealth of globalized society no longer presents itself as an immense or monstrous collection of commodities but as an equally formidable collection of financial securities, instead?[8] Or might it be, simply, that with the rise of securitization, something of the commodity form has come to mediate not only how we make the things we need (requiring us, that is, to treat labor power as a commodity in its own right), but also how we plan the very process of their production? And if that is indeed the case, what kind of relation or social bond is ultimately created by the generalization of the security form? What conditions does it presuppose, and what relations does it in turn create? We know already that the financial security, much like the commodity with which Marx began, presents itself at first as "an extremely obvious, trivial thing." But on close inspection, will we not find that it, too, is a very peculiar thing, "abounding in metaphysical subtleties and theological niceties"?[9]

THE TWO FACTORS OF THE SECURITY: USE VALUE AND HEDGING VALUE

Of the commodity, Marx wrote that it is first of all "an external object, a thing which through its qualities satisfies human needs of whatever kind."[10] Marx had in mind such things as wheat or iron, linen or coats, but the same could surely be said of the myriad bonds, stocks, and options that are being traded daily on the world's financial markets. After all, what is a municipal bond if not a financial instrument with which a city government might undertake the building of a new school or the repaving of an old road—or, from the standpoint of the subscriber, a way of investing in the city's welfare while simultaneously ensuring a modest but steady income for years to come?[11] Likewise, what are stocks, if not a way for industrialists to finance their productive activities without having to borrow from the bank or a way for investors to share in the potential profits generated by these activities? And what are wheat futures, if not a way for two parties—say, a miller and a farmer—to protect themselves from the potential fluctuations in the price of wheat or flour?[12]

From the first corporate shares issued by the Dutch East India Company in 1602 to the credit default swaps created by J. P. Morgan in 1994, the history of capitalism has been marked by the discovery and invention of countless new securities, each with its own specific uses. What is more, for several centuries, it has been common for these contracts to be traded as securities, either "over the counter" (as in the case of many financial derivatives) or in formal exchanges such as the Amsterdam or the New York Stock Exchanges.[13] And yet, as I have already intimated, something has undoubtedly changed in recent years in the character of both financial markets and the societies around them, where financial securities seem to be considered less and less for their specific usefulness (whether in financing a particular project or providing a certain income) and more and more for their value in exchange—or more precisely, for their value as hedges in the construction of a properly diversified portfolio. Thus, for instance, where an investor might once have acquired stock in a given company because she thought it would allow that company to undertake specific activities while also entitling her to a share of the resulting profits, the same investor today may well have purchased the stock chiefly as a way to offset the risks entailed by an earlier investment. As for the person who has just sold her the shares, meanwhile, he is likely to have done so not because he needed the money to invest in another project, but because he, too, was obeying the same imperative of maintaining a properly calibrated portfolio. At times, in fact, it appears as if securities were being produced in order merely to be exchanged or used as hedges for one another, as one contract calls forth another, which in turn calls forth another, and so on. In other words, in the incessant and generalized quest for the ever-more-diversified portfolio, it appears that today's securities are not only financial "use values," as Marx might have put it, but the "material bearers" of "exchange value"—or more precisely, perhaps, the material bearers of what we might call "hedging value."[14] But what is the nature of this value, one wonders? What is expressed through these exchanges, and what might the exchanges themselves accomplish?

When Marx began his own inquiry into the nature of value, the reader may remember, he began with two commodities in a relation of exchange—wheat (or "corn," as per Fowkes's translation) and iron, *Weizen und Eisen*—and asked what their equation signified (*Was*

> Let us now take two commodities, for example corn and iron. Whatever their exchange relation may be, it can always be represented by an equation in which a given quantity of corn is equated to some quantity of iron, for instance 1 quarter of corn = x cwt of iron. What does this equation signify? It signifies that a common element of identical magnitude exists in two different things, in 1 quarter of corn and similarly in x cwt of iron. Both are therefore equal to a third thing, which in itself is neither the one nor the other. Each of them, so far as it is exchange-value, must therefore be reducible to this third thing (Marx, *Capital*, vol. 1, p. 127)

besagt diese Gleichung?).[15] Marx's own answer to the question, sadly— whereby it is the socially necessary labor time required to produce commodities that accounts for their value—seems largely insufficient to explain the ups and downs or the hedging value of stocks and bonds, but the question itself remains suggestive. After all, what might it mean to say that the risk associated with a given investment—say, a purchase of 100 shares in a mining company—can be hedged by the acquisition of x iron ore futures, y shares in a solar energy company, or z treasury bonds? On some level, clearly, such assets are entirely incommensurable, and yet, manifestly, people on trading floors around the world are continually offsetting such bets one with the other—every day of the year, every hour of the day. What is it that these assets have in common and that allows them to be hedged for one another, and what is achieved as a result? Or to put it differently, what are the conditions that make such equivalences possible, and what conditions do these equivalences make possible in turn?

Since Marx began with wheat and iron, I propose that we begin with a couple of securities of our own—say, a wheat futures contract and a block of shares in a mining company—as they might appear in the portfolio of an imaginary investor. The wheat futures, first, we might think of as being useful to millers or farmers—or to anyone whose line of work somehow exposes them to the fluctuations in the price of wheat or flour. Thus, we can conceive of a miller, for instance, who—having invested much of his money in the construction of a new mill—now finds himself especially vulnerable to potential changes in the price of wheat. Faced with this uncertainty, thankfully, our miller has the option of entering into a contract with someone else, locking in the price of wheat and thereby hedging the risk he incurred by purchasing the mill in the first place. Such a contract, of course, does not mean that he has eliminated the risks of doing business with wheat, but it does mean that he has found someone else—a farmer, perhaps, or a baker—with whom to share them. Or more precisely, it means that he has found through the intercession of the futures exchange a great many investors with whom to do so, at least potentially. Signing a futures contract is no guarantee of success, but together with the purchase of the mill, it is what makes it possible for him to take his chances at being a miller.

If we were now to ask after the value not of a wheat futures contract, but of a common stock, we might construct a similar scenario whereby an entrepreneur decides to take his company public. Who knows: perhaps he wants to finance the company's operations without having to borrow money from the bank or use his equipment as collateral. Perhaps he wants to create a more diversified portfolio for himself by reducing his exposure to the ups and downs of that particular business. (After all, once he has sold some of his shares in one company, nothing should stop him from acquiring a stake in a rival company, thereby separating his personal fortune from that of his original company.) Whatever his reasons, one thing is certain: by taking his company public, this private investor is taking something of a risk, since he is now leaving his fate—at least in part—to the ups and downs of the stock market. At the same time, however, this is the kind of risk that will allow him to take other risks—since it allows him, say, to develop new products or seek new markets—and these in turn are risks that he is ultimately sharing with all those who have acquired (or might acquire) his newly issued shares.

From the standpoint of those purchasing the stock, meanwhile (just as from the standpoint of the farmer who took the other end of the futures contract), the wager is much the same: by acquiring shares, new investors are exposing themselves to potential fluctuations in the stock price, which in turn depend on the activities of countless other traders. At any given moment, thousands of shares of the same company are likely being bought and sold, causing the price to go up or down, and in addition to this, countless shares in other companies are also being traded, indirectly affecting both the price and the volatility of the initial stock.

The conclusion of all this may be stated simply: in the end, whether in the case of the mining stock or of the wheat futures, the price, volatility, and what I am calling the hedging value of a security are a function not just of the original wager made by the investor or by the miller who initially signed the contract, but of the incessant speculative activity of *all* market players. Indeed—and therein lies the paradoxical nature of liquidity as both the condition and the ultimate promise of efficient markets—it is only because the fluctuating prices of securities are assumed to reflect or express the activity of the market in general that

> It might seem that if the value of a commodity is determined by the quantity of labour expended to produce it, it would be the more valuable the more unskillful and lazy the worker who produced it, because he would need more time to complete the article. However, the labour that forms the substance of value is equal human labour, the expenditure of identical human labour-power. The total labour-power of society, which is manifested in the values of the world of commodities, counts here as one homogeneous mass of human labour-power, although composed of innumerable individual units of labour-power. (Marx, *Capital*, vol. 1, p. 129)

securities can be hedged for one another. And conversely, it is only to the extent that securities are indeed being hedged for one another that their fluctuating prices can be trusted to reflect the countless visions of the future that, together, make up the market as a whole.[16]

In a word, then, just as Marx once insisted it is the labor of all society that is expressed in the relation of commodities in exchange, it would appear that a similar logic is at work in today's financial markets. There, the value of financial securities as hedges, at least according to contemporary financial economics, can be said to derive from all the mutual promises they represent—or more precisely, perhaps, from the amount of risk that these promises contain.[17] On some basic level, indeed, it is fairly obvious that financial securities contain an element of risk, in the sense that their price could go up or down. But no less importantly, financial securities can also be said to contain risk in another sense, since—precisely to the extent that they expose their owners to the fluctuations of a specific asset price—they may also be used to help mitigate (or "contain") the risks entailed by other investments. How much risk an individual security contains may be a more complicated matter, but something of Marx's reasoning should still apply. And just as Marx thought the exchange value of commodities depends on the amount of socially necessary labor time required to produce or reproduce them, perhaps we may find—at the risk of oversimplifying—that the hedging value of financial securities depends similarly on the amount of risk that is required to reproduce them, or more accurately (as we will see), on the amount of risk one must take in order to *replicate* them.

THE RISE OF MODERN FINANCIAL THEORY (MARKOWITZ, SHARPE)

The theory of value just outlined, implausible though it may seem, is not entirely unlike the theory of value that underpins contemporary financial economics. Before the early decades of the twentieth century, the value of a security was understood not in terms of risk, but

> It seemed obvious that investors are concerned with risk and return, and that these should be measured for the portfolio as a whole. Variance (or, equivalently, standard deviation) came to mind as a measure of risk of the portfolio. The fact that the variance of the portfolio, that is the variance of a weighted sum, involved all covariance terms added to the plausibility of the approach. Since there were two criteria—expected return and risk—the natural approach for an economics student was to imagine the investor selecting a point from the set of Pareto optimal expected return, variance of return combinations, now known as the efficient frontier. These were the basic elements of portfolio theory which appeared one day while reading Williams. (Harry Markowitz, "Foundations of Portfolio Theory," 1990)

as a function of its expected return. On this view, two securities such as a wheat futures contract and a block of shares in a mining company were considered equivalent (that is, equal in value) if they had the same expected return.[18] Starting in the 1950s, however, such an account became untenable. As Harry Markowitz pointed out, if an investor conceived of the value of a security only as its expected return (even if he took pains to estimate the confidence in his projections), he would find himself selecting only those securities that promised the highest expected return, without regard to anything else. "If you are in love with IBM," as Peter Bernstein puts it, "why own Apple Computer and Digital Equipment, too? Why, in fact, own General Electric or Consolidated Edison at the same time you own IBM?"[19] But this is clearly not how investors think in the real world, as Markowitz pointed out, nor is it how they should think and act. Investors do (and should) consider not only expected return (which is a "desirable thing"), but also the uncertainty or variance of return (which is an "undesirable thing").

In order to determine whether a given asset should be included in her portfolio, then, an investor would need to assess not only the expected returns on that particular asset, but also the variance of these returns—or more precisely, their covariance with those of every other asset in her portfolio. Better yet, and more expediently, for sure, the investor would need to calculate the relation of that asset to what William Sharpe, a graduate student of Harry Markowitz's, posited as a dominant factor with which the movement of all securities was assumed to correlate.[20] That factor "could be 'the level of the stock market as a whole, the Gross National Product, some price index,'" or something else, "but it must be 'a factor thought to be the most important single influence on the return from securities.'"[21] Thus, the reasoning went, the investor would be able to determine whether including a specific asset in her portfolio would add to her overall risk (if the volatility of the asset's price was deemed greater than that of the dominant factor) or, on the contrary, make her portfolio comparatively less risky (if the volatility of the asset was less than that of the dominant factor).

Although unrelated in most every way to anything Marx ever wrote, Sharpe's contribution to modern portfolio theory bears at least some resemblance to Marx's understanding of value. In his analysis of commodities, the reader may recall, Marx observes that when we exchange

> If we leave aside the determinate quality of productive activity, and therefore the useful character of the labour, what remains is its quality of being an expenditure of human labour-power. Tailoring and weaving, although they are qualitatively different productive activities, are both a productive expenditure of human brains, muscles, nerves, hands etc., and in this sense both human labour. They are merely two different forms of the expenditure of human labour-power. (Marx, *Capital*, vol. 1, p. 134)

the products of our labor as commodities, that is, when we treat products of labor as products for exchange, we not only abstract from the use values of these particular commodities, we also abstract from the particular kinds of labor required or from the particular "concrete" labors of which they are they result. Thus, when we exchange twenty yards of linen and one coat as commodities, it is not as the products of weaving or sewing, but as the products of abstract human labor in general that they have value. Marx was understandably proud of his distinction between concrete and abstract labor—calling it a crucial point (*Springpunkt*) on which the understanding of political economy turned.[22] What it suggested was that the value of a given commodity is not the result of the particular concrete labor of an individual worker, nor is it determined merely by the amount of time that a particular worker actually spends making that specific commodity. It is, rather, a function of the average productivity of all workers—or, to use Marx's phrase—a function of the "socially necessary labour time" required to produce (or reproduce) such a commodity.

What Sharpe's analysis implies—though not in so many words—is that a similar kind of abstraction is at work in the exchange of financial securities. To illustrate, let us consider two new securities—say, an oil futures contract and stock in a high-tech company—and the

> On the one hand, all labour is an expenditure of human labour-power, in the physiological sense, and it is in this quality of being equal, or abstract, human labour that it forms the value of commodities. On the other hand, all labour is an expenditure of human labour-power in a particular form and with a definite aim, and it is in this quality of being concrete useful labour that it produces use-values. (Marx, *Capital*, vol. 1, p. 137)

way their price fluctuates as a function of world events. The price of oil, presumably—and hence the price of oil futures—is likely to change in response to political developments in the Middle East; the price of shares in a high-tech company, meanwhile, may be largely unaffected by such developments, but could react very sharply to news of a possible silicon shortage. These are known as "idiosyncratic risks"—risks associated with a particular firm or a particular sector. They are specific to each of these assets (much as sewing and weaving are specific to the coat and the linen) and are in a sense irreducible: there is nothing one can do to prevent the price of oil futures from changing when there is strife in the Middle East, just as there is nothing one can do to keep high-tech stocks from fluctuating in response to news of a silicon shortage. If one were to combine such disparate securities into one portfolio, however, one would find one's exposure to these particular risks reduced. In a properly constructed portfolio—or so the theory goes—the only risk left is the risk of holding the market portfolio (the so-called "market" or "systematic" risk). And the individual β of a given stock (that is, the sensitivity of its returns to changes in the underlying factor), therefore, can arguably be understood as resulting from the wagers being made by all market players—and not merely by those actively buying and selling that particular stock.

Ultimately, then, where Marx could plausibly contend in the nineteenth century that insofar as they are exchange values, "all commodities are merely definite quantities of *congealed labour-time*," so it would seem that in contemporary financial markets, financial securities

> Men do not therefore bring the products of their labour into relation with each other because they see these objects merely as the material integuments of homogeneous human labour. The reverse is true: by equating their different products to each other in exchange as values, they equate their different products to each other in exchange as values, they equate their different kinds of labour as human labour. They do this without being aware of it. (Marx, *Capital*, vol. 1, pp. 166–67)

have value as hedges insofar—and only insofar—as they are definite quantities of "congealed" *risk*. That is not to say, of course, that traders exchange securities because they think of them as congealed abstract risk, any more than the guardians of commodities in Marx's *Capital* exchanged their wares because they thought of them as "material integuments of homogeneous human labour." It is, rather, the reverse that is true (and, arguably, underpins the theory of efficient markets): as traders exchange financial securities on the market, they reduce them in actuality to what they have in common: risk. They may not know that they are doing it, but they are.[23]

"A UNIVERSAL FINANCIAL DEVICE"

So far, taking Marx as our guide, we have found that if there is such a thing as value that is somehow expressed in the hedging value of securities (while at the same time being hidden therein), it must be sought in the promise-making and speculative activity of all those who find themselves dealing and trading in securities. But if we are to follow Marx's reasoning further, there remains one more question to be addressed: If the value of securities does indeed derive from the risk they contain, how might we account for the peculiar way in which it appears on the financial markets themselves? How can it be, in other words, that the *social* character of risk—that is, the social character of risk taking and risk sharing among speculators—appears to them as it does, as relations between the securities themselves?

In his analysis of the commodity form and its generalization, Marx made the case that it was the emergence of a "universal equivalent"— the money commodity—that made it possible for the labor contained in all commodities to express itself as value while at the same time

> Now, however, we have to perform a task never even attempted by bourgeois economics. That is, we have to show the origin of this money-form, we have to trace the development of the expression of value contained in the value-relation of commodities from its simplest, almost imperceptible outline to the dazzling money-form. When this has been done, the mystery of money will immediately disappear. (Marx, *Capital*, vol. 1, p. 139)

making it seem that it was the things themselves—rather than the labor contained therein—that were somehow the source of value. Such an argument, while perhaps tenable in the nineteenth century, seems hardly applicable to today's financial markets, especially in the absence of a gold standard—or more generally, in the absence of any transcendental signifier against which the value of commodities and securities can be compared. And yet, interestingly, Marx's peculiar account of the emergence and importance of the money form is not without parallel in the stories that modern finance has been telling about itself and, in particular, about the rise of derivatives markets.

In broad strokes, the story goes something like this: Once upon a time, alongside traditional securities such as stocks and bonds, there existed a category of securities called "options." Options—as their name suggests—are a type of contract that gives individuals the option—but not the obligation—to purchase or sell a given asset (in the case

> The will of Alfred Nobel states, in part, that the Nobel Prize shall be awarded for an "important discovery or intervention." Fischer Black's and my discovery was how to price options and to provide a way to manage risk. Robert Merton developed an important alternative proof of the pricing technology and extended the approach in many directions including how to price options with dividends, how to price options when the interest rate is not constant, and how to apply a more general structure to price many other contingent contracts. (Myron Scholes, "Derivatives in a Dynamic Environment," 1997)

of a "call" or a "put," respectively) at a price set in advance, either by a certain date (in the case of American options) or on that date precisely (in the case of European options). Ownership of a stock option, for instance, might allow an individual to purchase shares in a given company at a price potentially well below market value—a most attractive prospect indeed—and making such options available, meanwhile, might be an inexpensive way for a start-up company to compensate its employees while simultaneously motivating them to work the requisite long hours.

It has long been evident that such contracts would be valuable to their owners (after all, there is no limit to the potential profit they could yield), but for most of their history, it was also difficult to determine precisely just *how* valuable—or more accurately, how such contracts should be priced.[24] Until recently, therefore, option contracts were used only rarely and even more rarely were they traded. And for good reason: when a bank did issue an options contract that had, say, three months to maturity, it had first to estimate the probable value of the underlying asset three months hence. It had also to average the probable value of the asset during the three-month period and, somehow, arrive at a plausible price at which to sell the option. This was a painstaking process that required both expertise and considerable guesswork, and there was no way of knowing in advance how accurate the pricing really was. Only when the option came to maturity would the contracting parties find out whether they had lost money, made money, or broken even.[25]

In the early 1970s, however, something of an "epistemological break" occurred that not only made it possible to price options in a more systematic fashion, but also contributed, as a result, to the radical transformation of financial markets. Indeed, this was a revolution that would change the very conception of what was being exchanged in these markets. By then, it should be noted, it was increasingly understood that stock prices evolve in a nonlinear fashion—or, more precisely, in a fashion that resembles Brownian motion.[26] From one moment to the next, the price of a stock could go up or down, it could change a lot or a little, but more likely than not, the price of a stock at one moment would be roughly the same as it had been the moment prior. Indeed, if one was thinking only in the very short term, all one needed to know in order to determine the probability distribution of a specific price at the next moment was the current price of the asset and its recent fluctuations.

With regard to the pricing of options—which, as the anthropologist Bill Maurer points out—are merely "a bet against the future price of a stock," what this meant was that the key to determining the value of an option would be simply "the price of the stock at time t and the temporal interval to time $t+1$."[27] More precisely, as Fischer Black and Myron Scholes put it in their landmark paper "The Pricing of Options and Corporate Liabilities," the value of the option could be shown to depend "only on the price of the stock and time and on variables that are taken to be known constants."[28] Indeed, as Black and Scholes realized, a bank issuing an option contract should be able to constitute a so-called "replicating portfolio" that, if maintained continuously throughout the duration of the contract (through the buying and selling of specific assets and the lending and borrowing of cash in appropriate quantities),

> Under these assumptions, the value of the option will depend only on the price of the stock and time and on variables that are taken to be known constants. Thus, it is possible to create a hedged position, consisting of a long position in the stock and a short position in the option, whose value will not depend on the price of the stock, but will depend only on time and the values of known constants. (Fischer Black and Myron Scholes, "The Pricing of Options and Corporate Liabilities," 1973)

should allow it to realize the contract exactly at a price set in advance. As the value of an option changes, so does the value of the underlying asset. Thus, "if the hedge is maintained continuously," as Black and Scholes reasoned, "the return on the hedged position is completely independent of the change in the value of the stock. In fact, the return on the hedged position becomes certain."[29] And, since the cost of this "replicating portfolio" can be determined in advance, it becomes possible for the option itself to be priced "scientifically."

As has been widely acknowledged, the Black-Scholes pricing formula was not the only important development in finance in the early 1970s. Only a couple of years earlier, Richard Nixon had suddenly put an end to a system of fixed exchange rates that had effectively functioned for several decades "as an open-ended American call and put option" (since, as Ole Bjerg points out, the existence of dollar-to-gold convertibility meant that the U.S. Treasury was ultimately "offering anyone 'the option but not the obligation' to exchange dollars for gold, or vice versa, at a given strike price at a given time in the future").[30] What is more, these were the years when the Chicago Mercantile

Exchange and the Chicago Board of Trade opened a market for currency futures and a market for trading in stock options, respectively. This was not the first time that derivatives were traded (indeed, in both of these marketplaces, people already had traded futures and other agricultural commodities in the nineteenth century), but the exchange of *financial* derivatives—that is, derivatives in which the underlying assets are themselves financial products, rather than physical commodities—was a novel development. And thanks in large part to the Black-Scholes pricing model, it was one that would expand dramatically, transforming people's understanding of what was ultimately being traded.[31] In the end, it might even be said that where the election of a single product of labor as universal equivalent was, according to Marx, what made possible the expression of the value contained in all products of labor (while at the same time concealing its origins in relations of production), the selection of the Black-Scholes formula is what allowed financial derivatives to serve as a "universal financial device" through which the speculative activity of the entire market could be expressed as volatility.[32] It was now possible for all participants in financial markets to take risks and bear them together, but to do so in such a way that the social character of these relations appeared to them in an inverted fashion, as a relation among securities themselves.

THE FETISHISM OF SECURITIES AND THE SECRET THEREOF

As we have already seen, financial securities appear at first blush as extremely obvious and trivial things. When the government of Brazil decides to issue ten-year or fifteen-year fixed-rate domestic bonds, for instance, it is merely committing to providing subscribers periodic interest payments until the bonds reach maturity. And if the resulting notes do offer a modicum of security to those who acquire them, it is clearly because these notes have the backing of the Brazilian government, which in turn depends on citizens and taxpayers to help it make good on its obligations. Similarly, when a bank chooses to securitize the debts it holds by issuing a collateralized debt obligation or similar asset-backed securities, all it is doing is promising to pass on what money it receives from its borrowers to investors, according

> A commodity appears at first sight an extremely obvious, trivial thing. But its analysis brings out that it is a very strange thing, abounding in metaphysical subtleties and theological niceties. So far as it is a use-value, there is nothing mysterious about it, whether we consider it from the point of view that by its properties it satisfies human needs, or that it first takes on these properties as the product of human labour. It is absolutely clear that, by his activity, man changes the forms of the materials of nature in such a way as to make them useful to him. The form of wood, for instance, is altered if a table is made out of it. Nevertheless the table continues to be wood, an ordinary, sensuous thing. But as soon as it emerges as a commodity, it changes into a thing which transcends sensuousness. It not only stands with its feet on the ground, but, in relation to all other commodities, it stands on its head, and evolves out of its wooden brain grotesque ideas, far more wonderful than if it were to begin dancing of its own free will. (Marx, *Capital*, vol. 1, pp. 163–64)

to a specific and explicit set of terms: a security with a AAA rating, for instance, will entitle its owner to receive his or her share of payments ahead of those who have purchased the BB-rated security, who in turn will receive their money ahead of those who have purchased "unsecured" tranches. There, too, it should be clear to anyone reading the contract that if the AAA-rated security is safe, it is not because it somehow contains only the mortgages of the most creditworthy borrowers. It does not. The security, rather, owes its rating or its appeal to the fact that it refers to a broad pool of mortgages and to the fact that other individuals, by investing in or holding on to lesser-rated securities, have been willing to absorb the first losses and thereby shoulder much of the risk of borrower default—for higher (potential) return. Just as the Brazilian bond derives its value not from the note itself, but from the government that issued it, the asset-backed securities, too, are valuable because of the myriad relations that make them possible.

And yet, as our analysis has also shown, that is not how things appear in financial markets. No sooner does a contract present itself as a security—that is to say, no sooner is it rated or priced as an asset to be traded or otherwise hedged—than something remarkable happens: the Brazilian treasury bonds themselves now appear as things of value—and not, as the term might once have implied, as "bonds" or relations between individuals who are seeking, together, to realize their respective ambitions. The AAA-rated and BB-rated securities, likewise, seem no longer to derive their value from the institutions that issued them—let alone from the complex mutualizing of risk that securitization simultaneously depends on and makes possible—but instead from the promises or promissory notes themselves.[33]

What is it, one wonders, that accounts for this phenomenon? Of what might it be a symptom and when—if ever—might we expect this mystification to disappear? In his analysis of the fetishism of commodities, Marx famously insisted that mystification is inseparable from the specific organization of production characteristic of capitalism. As soon as we arrive at another form of social organization, he argued, the "whole mystery" of the world of commodities disappears.[34] But what of the fetishism just described—this fetishism that attaches to promises and contracts when they are entered into as securities or as hedges for other contracts? It, too, it would seem, is specific to a certain mode of production—or more precisely, to a certain mode of prediction and protection characteristic of the contemporary capitalist organization of production in the North Atlantic zone. And indeed, we need only transport ourselves to societies different from our own—whether real or imagined—and we may find that "all the magic and necromancy" surrounding financial markets suddenly vanishes.[35]

Since economists today are no less fond of Robinsonades than they were in Marx's day, we may begin—like Marx—by transporting ourselves to Devil's Island and consider what we find there. On Devil's Island, the reader will recall, we find an individual by the name of

> As political economists are fond of Robinson Crusoe stories, let us first look at Robinson on his island. Undemanding though he is by nature, he still has needs to satisfy, and must therefore perform useful labours of various kinds; he must make tools, knock together furniture, tame llamas, fish, hunt and so on. Of his prayers and the like, we take no account here, since our friend takes pleasure in them and sees them as recreation. (Marx, *Capital*, vol. 1, p. 169)

Robinson Crusoe who—like any other—has various needs to satisfy. This particular lad, however, has the misfortune of living alone and having to do everything by and for himself. From the making of tools to the knocking together of furniture, from the taming of llamas to the procuring of food, Crusoe is forced to carry out "useful labors" of all kinds, useful labors that in any other setting would have been divided among a great number of individuals. It is a lonesome life, but it does offer one consolation: not only can Crusoe clearly distinguish among these various tasks, he can also see that these are but "different forms of activity of one and the same Robinson."[36] As a result, the relations between him and his products—"these objects that form his self-created wealth"—are entirely transparent and not, as they were back in the old country, shrouded in the mystifications of the market.[37]

There is more to Robinson Crusoe, however, than an obsessive concern with the making of tools and the procuring of food. After all, life on the island is full of dangers (and opportunities), and if he has any intention of producing or procuring the things he needs, part of his attention has to be devoted to planning for the future. And on close inspection, indeed, we find that if Crusoe is so adept at providing for his material needs, it is in part because he is so well attuned to the myriad dangers confronting him and to the diverse strategies he might adopt to deal with them. In particular, Crusoe is all too aware that he may not in fact be alone on the island, and when one December morning he sees signs of an encampment about two miles away, our hero knows that he had best ready himself for an attack. Anticipating what the savages might do to him if they ever were to find him, he takes all the necessary precautions: "I prepared myself within," he writes, "putting myself in a posture of defence. I loaded all cannon, as I called them, that is to say, my muskets, which were mounted upon my new fortification, and all my pistols, and resolved to defend myself to the last gasp; not forgetting seriously to commend myself to the Divine protection, and earnestly to pray to God to deliver me out of the hands of the barbarians."[38]

In his own reading of Defoe, interestingly, Marx noticed Crusoe's "prayers and the like," but immediately brushed them aside on the grounds that he took "pleasure in them" and saw them merely "as recreation." It may be true, I suppose, that if—like Marx—one concerns oneself only with Crusoe as a producer, his occasional prayer will seem irrelevant. But the fact is that Crusoe is not exclusively a laboring man, any more than he is purely a rationalist. As the above passage reminds us, he is also preoccupied with his physical safety and, like any reasonable Englishman of the seventeenth century, he will make sure to turn to God for extra assurance. And in many ways, more than a sign of some misplaced religiosity, these prayers may be seen instead as a testament to his resourcefulness. Crusoe evidently knows to protect himself against possible threats in a diversity of ways, making sure to prepare his muskets and pistols in anticipation of possible attacks, but adding a prayer or two, as well—just in case. And what is more, Crusoe's willingness to recommend himself to God's benevolence could well have less to do with any strong belief in the almighty than with an awareness—an awareness that seems all too rare among present-day experts in risk management—of the inevitable limits to our knowledge of the future. Crusoe, let us not forget, is a near contemporary of Blaise Pascal (the latter died only two years before Defoe was born). Like him, he knows a thing or two about probability theory, and like him, he knows also that there are things he does not know. Or perhaps he is simply the betting type and has wagered on God's existence. After all, as with a well-crafted derivative contract, the cost of a daily prayer is fairly minimal, but the potential payoff is limitless.[39]

Along these lines, we might also recall how Crusoe describes the night when, unexpectedly, a bolt of lightning struck the island: "I was not so much surprised with the lightning," he writes, "as I was with the thought which darted into my mind as swift as the lightning itself—Oh, my powder! My very heart sank within me when I thought that at one blast, all my powder might be destroyed."[40] Indeed, the storm impresses him to such an extent that once it is over, Crusoe puts everything else aside and applies himself "to make bags and boxes, to separate the powder, and to keep it a little and a little in a parcel in the hope that, whatever might come, it might not all take fire at once; and to keep it so apart that it should not be possible to make one part fire another."[41] In other words, Crusoe readily understands both the problem of risk and the management thereof, and within two weeks of the storm, the 240 pounds of powder have been "divided in not less than a hundred parcels."[42] I do not think Markowitz himself would have done any better.

If Defoe were to cast his hero on a desert island today, I suppose, he would likely make sure to acquaint him with the latest in quantitative risk analysis. At the very least, Crusoe would certainly take the time at the end of the day to calculate his "value at risk," assessing the probability of a specified loss of value to his portfolio of assets.[43] But the truth is, even if in addition to the pen, the ledger, and the watch, Crusoe were able to salvage the ship's more recent technologies (be it a hazmat suit, a high-definition surveillance camera, or a hand-held calculator preprogrammed with Black-Scholes model values and hedge ratios), our castaway would soon discover that these devices are of little use to him outside of his native England. Even more than the watch, in fact, these technologies would confront him as relics of the "risk society" he had left behind, and Crusoe would have to find other ways of combining—MacGyver-like—the skills and talents of the secret agent, the epidemiologist, and the risk manager.[44] Perhaps he would find that his safety and his foresight are diminished as a result, but he would at least be free of old illusions: no longer dreaming of bringing the future under his control, Crusoe would now recognize the fences around his encampment for what they are—the material and present trace of an imagined array of possible futures.

At this point, our travels can certainly be extended even further, but if from Robinson's island, "bathed in light," we now transported ourselves "to medieval Europe, shrouded in darkness," what would we find? According to Marx, "instead of the independent man," we would

> Let us now transport ourselves from Robinson's island, bathed in light, to medieval Europe, shrouded in darkness. Here, instead of the independent man, we find everyone dependent—serfs and lords, vassals and suzerains, laymen and clerics. Personal dependence characterizes the social relations of material production as much as it does the other spheres of life based on that production. But precisely because relations of personal dependence form the given social foundation, there is no need for labour and its products to assume a fantastic form different from their reality. They take the shape, in the transactions of society, of services in kind and payments in kind. (Marx, *Capital*, vol. 1, p. 170)

find "everyone dependent—serfs and lords, vassals and suzerains, laymen and clerics."[45] The "social relations of material production" under feudalism were indeed characterized by "personal dependence," according to Marx, which is why there was "no need for labour and its products to assume a fantastic form different from their reality."[46] Before the generalization of the money form, labor and its products could appear as "services in kind and payments in kind." And though it may be possible, in retrospect, to describe something like the medieval *corvée* in terms of the amount of labor time it required, the medieval serf certainly knew very well that what he was expending was a specific quantity of his own labor power. He did not need a daily wage from his lord to understand this. Likewise, he also realized what terrible privations the Church asked of him as a down payment for his possible salvation. As Marx put it with inimitable wit, "the tithe owed to the priest is more clearly apparent than his blessing."[47]

It may be interesting to note, once again, that much as he had dismissed Robinson's "prayers and the like" as mere entertainment, Marx seems to think of the blessing of the priest as immaterial—a mere pretext for the Church's very real acts of extortion. This is perhaps not surprising, given Marx's relentless focus on production and his equally insistent disdain for religion, but I wonder: Though the priest's blessing may be less tangible than the product of the serf's labor, is it any less real as a result? And from the standpoint of a medieval serf, does it not represent a very real form of protection—an assurance of salvation in another world, which can be obtained only in exchange for a proper contribution?

Medieval society—or so historians tell us—imagined itself as being composed of three orders: there were those who fought (the *bellatores*, or *pugnatores*), those who prayed (*oratores*), and those who worked (*laboratores*). Each order had its place and purpose, and just as "the function of the pure was to pray for their fellows, and that of the valiant was to risk their lives in defense of all, so the function of those whose value consisted in their weariness was to win the bread of other men in the sweat of their brow."[48] But if there clearly existed a unique division of labor characteristic of medieval society (or what Georges Duby persuasively calls a "seigneurial mode of production"), presumably this division of labor governed not only how people produced the goods they needed to survive, but how they prepared themselves for the future, anticipating what it might hold and protecting themselves against misfortune.[49] After all, medieval laborers knew as well as anyone else that merely providing for one's needs could be treacherous business, full of uncertainties and possible mishaps. But luckily for them, they knew also that in exchange for their toil, they could count on the priests and the knights to provide both "the salvation of their souls and the security of their bodies." Likewise, the *bellatores*, though they put their own bodies and souls in great peril, knew that they could count on the work of the *laboratores* to save them from starvation and on the good offices of the *oratores* to "cleanse them of the sins they commit by their arms."[50] And the *oratores*, finally, presumably trusted that they could at least satisfy some of their earthly desires in the safety of the monastery, so long as in exchange, they devoted some of their prayers to the salvation of other souls. Even at the time, in other words, the interdependence underpinning this seigneurial mode of protection was clearly understood and did not have to be disavowed. As one medieval bishop put it, "every legitimate royal throne stands on three columns, *oratores*, *laboratores*, *bellatores*." And as Georges Duby further makes clear, it was apparent to all that if one of these columns should buckle, "the throne would totter, and that if one of them gave way, it would collapse."[51]

CONCLUSION: AN ASSOCIATION OF FREE MEN?

The last stop in Marx's thought experiment, with which we ourselves may conclude, is "an association of free men" holding the means of production in common and "expending their many different forms of labour-power in full self-awareness as one single social labour force."[52] In such a society, as Marx points out, the characteristics of Robinson's labor would all be repeated, with the important difference that they would be "social instead of individual."[53] Thus, where

Robinson's products were manifestly the result of his personal labor alone and were of use only to him as an individual, the "total product" of our imagined association of free men would be a "social product," and transparently so. As Marx ventures, in fact, "the social relations of

> Let us finally imagine, for a change, an association of free men, working with the means of production held in common, and expending their many different forms of labour-power in full self-awareness as one single social labour force. All the characteristics of Robinson's labour are repeated here, but with the difference that they are social instead of individual. (Marx, *Capital*, vol. 1, p. 171)

the individual producers, both towards their labour and the products of their labour" would be "transparent in their simplicity" in both production and distribution.[54] Or to put it differently, there would be no need for the "magic and necromancy" that envelops those societies where the capitalist mode of production is dominant. Once it becomes production by "freely associated men" and once it stands "under their conscious and planned control," the process of material production no longer needs to be shrouded in a veil, and the fetishism of commodities can disappear.[55]

What Marx did not say, but what can be presumed, is that a world where people decide together on what is to be produced is also a world where people decide together on what possibilities are to be pursued, what dangers are to be avoided, what risks are worth taking. In such a society, in other words, the means of prediction and protection would also be held in common, and the fetishism I have been describing—the fetishism of securities—would also disappear. But when and where might such a society ever be found? On one reading of *Capital*, it does seem that Marx's "association of free men" belongs somewhere in the future—and in a distant future, at that. But is it necessarily so? Must this promise always be postponed, or could it be that the freedom

Marx evokes is closer at hand than we think? Marx himself was able to travel to Devil's Island and to medieval Europe—at least in his imagination—and from there returned to the reading room of the British Museum. This did not alter the historical conditions under which he labored, nor did it loosen the grip of the market on the lives of his contemporaries. But one may reasonably wonder, nonetheless, if only as a result of Marx's own analysis: Is the generalization of the commodity form as complete and ineluctable as Marx's story seems to imply, or could it be that Marx's point—or at the very least, one implication of his analysis—is that we do in fact retain the power to resist and interrupt the reduction or abstraction of all social relations to a mere question of value?

Looking back on the detail of our own narrative in the preceding pages—a narrative that hewed fairly closely to Marx's own, we might note that we began not with an individual security in isolation, but with several securities as they appeared in the portfolio or on the computer screen of an imaginary trader. From an examination of the relations among these securities, we arrived at the conclusion that if indeed they have value as hedges, it is insofar as they "contain" risk in various ways. Having thus identified the source or substance of hedging value in the speculative activity of all market players, we traced our way back to its appearance as volatility. Where Marx traced the development of the money form, we proposed that the development of the Black-Scholes options-pricing formula and the resulting expansion of the derivatives market were what made possible both the generalized exchange of volatility and its expression as value in the peculiar idiom of contemporary finance.[56]

At each step of the way—again, like Marx—we returned to the same relation of exchange between securities to introduce new distinctions. Or did we really? After all, just as Marx's analysis used up a good number of commodities, from wheat and iron to linen and coats, shoe polish and dancing tables, our own analysis moved through a certain number of examples, from wheat futures to asset-backed securities. Why the change of examples? And why these particular securities? To some extent, the choice of assets was dictated by the needs of the argument. Thus, for instance, the combination of oil futures and shares in a high-tech company seemed more helpful for illustrating the notions of idiosyncratic and market risk than would have been, say, shares in IBM and Apple Inc.. But to be honest, I had also hoped that some of these examples might help convey the strangeness—indeed, the absurdity—of contemporary financial markets. As Marx points out toward the end of *Capital*'s opening chapter, "if I state that coats or boots stand in a relation to linen because the latter is the universal incarnation of abstract labour, the absurdity of the statement is self-evident."[57] And yet, as Marx also points out, "when the producers of coats and boots bring these commodities into a relation with linen, or with gold or silver... as the universal equivalent, the relation between their own private labour and the collective labour of society appears to them in exactly this absurd form." Indeed, the "categories of bourgeois economics consist precisely of forms of this kind."[58]

Today, if I were to claim that the likelihood of a Greek government default stands in a relation—any relation—to the likelihood of a hurricane flooding the city of Orlando, the absurdity of the claim would also be manifest. Yet as our own analysis suggests, the categories of contemporary financial economics consist of precisely such absurdities. When private fund managers or government agencies enter into credit default swaps or acquire catastrophe bonds ("CAT bonds") in order to hedge the risks entailed by other investments (say, in Greek government bonds or in shares of SeaWorld Parks and Entertainment), it is the relation between their own risks and the collective risk-taking activity of society that confronts them in the same absurd form. It may be, I suppose, that the traders on the floor or the risk managers in the back office share some sense that "in the last instance" (to borrow a phrase from Louis Althusser), the only risks to be concerned with are those that threaten the creation and appropriation of surplus value. After all, even the most exotic weather derivative will refer to a specific "event," and most events are unlikely even to register as such—at least in a capitalist universe—unless they are of some concern to some producer, somewhere. At the same time, however, it also seems that over the years, we have allowed ourselves to proceed as if all these risks were not only natural categories, but entirely commensurable, and we have even trained ourselves—or those who trade our pension funds on our behalf—to treat such equivalences as natural and inevitable, almost necessary. The difference between events or between securities does not disappear, of course—on the contrary—but it confronts us only as a difference on the screen: a difference of value, a possibility for arbitrage, but not a question of meaning.[59] What is it, one has to wonder, that hides behind these exchanges? What do these equations signify? What makes them possible, and what do they make possible in turn? As computerized, high-frequency trading comes to supplant the deliberate judgment of individual traders, these questions are no doubt increasingly difficult. They are also more important than ever. It is to these questions we now turn.

CHAPTER THREE

Finding Safety in Numbers:
Inside the Hidden Abode of Prediction

After having finally solved the mystery of value—a mystery that he contended had confounded the human mind "for more than 2,000 years," Marx in 1867 accompanied his friend Moneybags (*Geldbesitzer*) to the market, hoping to solve another mystery. The mystery went something like this: On the one hand, it was a basic law of political economy that markets are fair. Commodities on average were thought to be exchanged at their value, which was itself understood to be a function of how much labor is required to produce them (or, as Marx would have it, of how much socially necessary labor time is required to produce them). On the other hand, Moneybags—who had never worked so much as a day in his life—seemed to be accumulating more and more money for himself. Money was being exchanged for commodities (M–C) and commodities were being exchanged for money (C–M'), but by the end of the process, it seemed that more value was being generated than had been put into circulation (M' = M + ΔM). How was this possible? What was the nature of this expanding wealth, and what was its magical source?

When Marx followed Moneybags to the market and saw what he was buying, the mystery quickly lifted. Moneybags, Marx discovered, was "lucky enough" to find in circulation a special commodity—a commodity the use value of which possessed "the peculiar property of being a source of value," a commodity "whose actual consumption" was "therefore itself an objectification of labour, hence a creation of value."[1] This commodity was none other than people's "labouring capacity" or "labour power," as Marx famously called it. The value of this labor power, like that of any other commodity, was determined by the amount of labor time required to produce it, but since a worker could, over the course of a day, produce more than he needed to reproduce the blood and sweat he had expended that day, by purchasing and using up the labor power of others, the money owner could hope to generate more value than the wage cost him in the first place. Thus, Marx could claim to have found both the source and true nature of capitalist wealth in the exploitation by one person—fair and square—of another person's fundamental human needs: on the one hand, a source of increasing power for the few, on the other, a source of great vulnerability for the many.

A century and a half later, there is a certain quaintness to Marx's critique of value. For one thing, there is hardly a mainstream economist around who still speaks of "labor" as the source of value, and Marx's critique of the classical paradigm partly misfires as a result.[2] For another, even the most vulgar Marxists have had to acknowledge that while capitalists are clearly employing and exploiting workers in all corners of the world, from the United States to Mexico and from China to Bangalore, profits in the so-called "capitalist core" derive mostly from financial activities.[3] In these countries, in fact, it almost seems Moneybags is less interested in hiring people than in lending them money or helping them place their modest savings in a volatile stock market. Moneybags is doing just fine, mind you, and the ultimate source of his wealth (or the ultimate victim of its expansion) may be the same, but his appearance has changed: no longer the portly bourgeois in a top hat, as in a Daumier lithograph, our friend now has the more dashing figure of a Leonardo DiCaprio in *The Wolf of Wall Street*.[4]

As antiquated as Marx's categories may appear, however, there is also much about his line of questioning that remains pertinent to this day. In the nineteenth century, as we have seen, Marx wondered (or feigned to wonder) how it was possible for the mere exchange of commodities—the buying and selling of products of human labor—to generate so much wealth for some and so much misery for the others. But is there not today a similar question haunting our discussions of financial markets? After all, how are we to make sense of the ever-expanding trade in financial securities, and how can we explain that such a trade should create such extraordinary power for our handsome financier while creating increasing vulnerability for so many of us?

On some level, the answer may be ready at hand: finance is but the form taken by present-day capital, and the extraordinary riches that are accruing to the financier are but the result of his having claimed as his own the fruits of other people's labors (past, present, or future). But while this surely holds in broad outlines, there is another wrinkle to the story. As I have already intimated, it seems that in the twenty-first century, as in the nineteenth, we are asked to believe that markets are equitable and efficient in their distribution of resources.[5] Adam Smith certainly thought so, and Eugene Fama—the much-maligned, much-celebrated author of the efficient market hypothesis (and recent recipient of a Nobel Prize in Economics), has similarly maintained that markets are "informationally efficient," meaning that stock prices at any given moment can be assumed to reflect all the available information about individual stocks and the market as a whole.[6] If someone had privileged information about a stock and were to trade accordingly, the reasoning goes, the share price would instantaneously adjust to reflect this inside information, thereby effectively rendering it public and available to anyone. From this it follows that there is no such thing as "riskless profit" (or, in the idiom of finance, no possibility of "arbitrage"), meaning that no one is able consistently to game the system. Or as the economist Paul Samuelson once quipped, "it is not easy to become rich in Las Vegas, Churchill Downs or the local Merrill Lynch office."[7] And yet, even in this ostensibly zero-sum game where one person's gain is always matched by another person's loss, it would appear that the local Merrill Lynch office is thriving, thank you very much, and this seemingly by virtue simply of trading in financial securities. How is one to explain this peculiar phenomenon? That Moneybags is smiling, that much is clear: laughing, even. But what lies behind his unnerving smile, what is the secret of his eerie laughter?

Taking another leaf out of Marx's playbook, I propose in this chapter to follow Moneybags to the market once again—to the financial market, this time—and to examine what he finds there. More precisely, I will consider what he has found there over the last thirty-odd years in the United States, where—as we have already seen in Chapter 2— a great deal has changed in how he approaches financial matters. Moneybags has long dabbled in finance, of course, lending and investing here and there, and Marx himself certainly acknowledged the importance of these activities in the capitalist mode of production.[8] But where Moneybags once lent money only sparingly and to the safest of borrowers, it now seems he is lending with abandon, sending credit cards to just about anyone with a pulse (or a credit record), and offering mortgages to even the most "subprime" of borrowers. What is more, where in the past the moneylender would hold on to borrowers' promissory notes until their debts were paid in full, it seems now that he is as eager to part with these debts as he is to acquire them. And this is true in other areas of finance, too: investors who once prided themselves in poring over the fundamentals of a company before committing any money, selecting only those few blue-chip stocks that would yield steady returns, are now happy to select a whole panoply of stocks and bonds—including often the junkiest of junk bonds—which they proceed to sell just as quickly, depending not on their long-term prospects, but on their level of volatility. Today's investor, in other words, seems to have thrown caution to the wind, abandoning all the principles he once held dear. And who can blame him? The resulting profits are unprecedented, far in excess of any returns he could have obtained from investing directly in production.

As I have already suggested and as I will try to document further in the present chapter, the transformation and marketization of American finance in the late twentieth century is inseparable from changing conceptualizations and measures of financial risk. Looking first at the case of consumer lending in the United States, we will see how the development of new techniques for measuring the risk of borrower default has made it possible for Moneybags to lend more money than ever before. Then, by considering the rise of mortgage-backed securities, we will see how the generalization of these techniques has also made it possible for Moneybags to borrow more money than ever before—contributing along the way to the emergence of market-based finance.[9] The result is nothing short of extraordinary, as if Moneybags had—once again—discovered a miraculous commodity: one that, like labor power, he can acquire on the fairest of terms while simultaneously deriving strength from the transaction. Since at least the nineteenth century, arguably, Moneybags has been able to purchase other people's labor power at its value while somehow generating more value through the mere act of using it. But as we will see, it appears that Moneybags or a relation of his is now similarly able to claim other people's credibility or probability—that is, their ability to be believed—while himself becoming miraculously more credible as a result. Ultimately, it may be that what Moneybags has found are but the same vulnerable people as before—or more precisely, the same vulnerability as before—and that there is in fact nothing new under the sun. But as we will see, the terms of the relationship between Moneybags and those he encounters (or more precisely, the terms of the relationship that "Moneybags" is allowed here to represent) have undoubtedly changed, and as such, they are deserving of their own critique.

A NEW CONCEPTION OF CREDITWORTHINESS

When Moneybags goes to market, the story goes, he finds a "free worker," an individual who is free to alienate his or her labor power in exchange for a wage, but has effectively no choice but to do so.[10] Or rather, I should say, he finds countless such individuals—many

> For the transformation of money into capital, therefore, the owner of money must find the free worker available on the commodity-market; and this worker must be free in the double sense that as a free individual he can dispose of his labour-power as his own commodity, and that, on the other hand, he has no other commodity for sale, i.e. he is rid of them, he is free of all the objects needed for the realization of his labour-power. (Marx, *Capital*, vol. 1, pp. 272–73)

more than he has jobs to offer, and it is the existence of this "industrial reserve army" of the unemployed that gives Moneybags the upper hand.[11] But even this picture needs to be complicated, for in many parts of the world, both in advanced economies and in parts of the developing world, the individuals Moneybags finds are not simply in search of a job. They are also in search of credit. Some of them, in fact, are so desperate that they need a loan simply to buy their groceries. Others may have a reasonably steady job, but their wages have fallen so low that they are chronically behind in their rent and in desperate need of a cushion. Others yet, of course, may have done very well for themselves, but they have aspirations of doing even better—whether by becoming first-time home owners, say, or by using an existing home to get a loan with which to buy another.

For most of the history of modern capitalism, when someone approached him in search of a loan, Moneybags would take one kind of approach. In the United States, for instance, he would ask prospective borrowers about their employment, their marital status and churchgoing habits, and so on, and occasionally, he might even inquire with the neighbors. This allowed him somehow to get at the applicants' creditworthiness—a feature that he took to be immanent to the person, akin to their character or perhaps their soul. Moneybags

> A rich man gives credit to a poor man whom he considers industrious and decent. This kind of credit belongs to the romantic, sentimental part of political economy, to its aberrations, excesses, exceptions, not to the rule. But even assuming this exception and granting this roman-tic possibility, the life of the poor man and his talents and activity serve the rich man as a guarantee of the repayment of the money lent. That means, therefore, that all the social virtues of the poor man, the content of his vital activity, his existence itself, represent for the rich man the reimbursement of his capital with the customary interest. (Marx, *Comments on James Mill, MECW*, vol. 3, p. 215)

was an honest judge of character, in other words, not unlike George Bailey—Jimmy Stewart's eminently likable character in Frank Capra's *It's a Wonderful Life*, who was willing and able to lend most generously to those whom he knew to be trustworthy.

In the early twentieth century in the United States, however, a new set of practices began to emerge that would change both the char-acter of the information being collected and, eventually, the kind of knowledge (and power) thus created. Around 1917, mail-order com-panies—unable to interview applicants directly—had the idea of giv-ing applicants forms to fill out. At around the same time, as Donncha Marron explains, department stores such as Sears and Spiegler's began similarly to grant (or deny) credit on the basis not of interviews, but of people's answers to questionnaires.[12] In terms of content, the nature of the information being gathered was roughly the same as before (that is, the questions might still pertain to a person's mari-tal status, employment history, and so on), but the data were being collected in different ways and took a different form—one that would one day make them amenable to new kinds of analysis. Specifically, instead of the narratives written by the assessor, Moneybags was now coding applicants' responses in binary terms, accumulating files that would later be mined for predictive purposes and used as the basis for lending algorithms.

In addition to gathering information about applicants in novel ways, moneylenders in the 1920s and 1930s also started to gather and share information about people who had already been granted credit. In the United States, lenders started communicating the names of those borrowers who had defaulted on their debts to the newly devised "credit bureaus," which in turn would make the information available to other lenders (for a fee), helping them determine which loans should be extended or which ones should be renewed. When someone turned up as having defaulted on a loan in the past, this was usually taken as a sign that this person was a bad payer, and on the basis of this perceived character trait, they were likely to be denied their next loan. The notion of creditworthiness was thus initially unchanged, in that it was still considered an immanent attribute of a person, but as credit bureaus started to gather and share more and more information in newly systematic ways, a new kind of thinking became possible, which all but changed the meaning of creditworthiness. Thus, in 1941, the economist David Durand at the National Bureau of Economic Research had the idea of using the data gathered by various institutional lenders over the years and of comparing the information provided by applicants with their subsequent payment history as borrowers, searching for potential patterns that might help lenders predict default among prospective borrowers.[13] As Marron puts it, a new statistical "imaginary" was thus born in which a probabilistic model could be used to determine who should receive credit and who should not.[14] And indeed, as historical data continued to accumulate—including not only the information the borrowers revealed at the time of their credit application, but also the detail of how they fared over the duration of the loan, analysts were able to develop models that, "when applied to individuals, produced a predictive, probabilistic statement as to the calculated likelihood, or 'risk,' of default."[15]

THE RISE OF THE CREDIT SCORE

While the rise of mail-order companies and the development of credit bureaus is what helped transform the world of consumer finance in the first half of the twentieth century, it is the subsequent invention and expansion of the credit card in the latter half of the century that most significantly helped the development of this new statistical imaginary and led to its extension to areas outside of consumer finance.[16] Already in 1949, as Marron chronicles, the introduction of the Diners Club card meant that credit was no longer negotiated or allocated at the site of consumption, which in turn meant not only that the dramatis personae of the credit relation had changed (money was now being lent by external players), but that the decisions governing the allocation of credit were now being made at a distance and according to increasingly abstract and bureaucratic procedures. What is more, as the use of credit cards became generalized and electronic credit networks expanded, a new "avalanche" of numbers (to borrow Ian Hacking's phrase) opened up possibilities for new ways of governing credit.[17] Much as Durand in the 1940s had constructed his initial predictive model on the basis of information gathered by institutional lenders, by the 1980s, the company Fair, Isaac had the idea of using credit histories recorded by one of the three credit bureaus, Experian, to devise a "scoring" device—what would become known as the FICO score—the purpose of which was to help in the interpretation of an individual's credit history.[18] The function of the score was to express as a numerical figure an individual's probability of default. The score was thus specific to each individual and was based on that particular individual's credit history, which was continuously updated. At the same time, however, it was also calculated through an analysis of all the data available—not just of that particular individual's history.

The FICO score, however imperfect, was quickly picked up by the other two bureaus, which decided to offer this score to their clients alongside the individuals' credit histories. As a result, in a matter of years, each of the two hundred million individuals tracked by these three bureaus in the United States could be scored in terms of their risk or probability—through a technology that not only expressed as a single numerical figure the result of a comparative analysis of everyone's credit histories, but that also made it possible, in turn, for lenders, landlords, and so on, to compare prospective borrowers, renters and the like along an axis of creditworthiness—or, more precisely, to compare them in terms of their relative risk of default. By the 1990s, the FICO score had effectively come to serve as a measure of individuals' creditworthiness and of the risk associated with holding their debt—and this despite the fact that creditworthiness had traditionally been thought of as "a personal property of the individual" akin to character, rather than a "shifting quality" determined statistically with reference to aggregate populations.[19]

The significance of the score is hard to overstate, but it is also hard to articulate precisely. One consequence of these new techniques, quite simply, was that Moneybags was now better at predicting default, meaning that he could be more precise or more judicious in his choice of borrowers: he could steer clear of those prospective borrowers who would likely default, and some of those applicants who might have been once considered "too risky" could now be turned into profitable investments. Thanks to the right amount of deregulation, indeed, Moneybags could now tailor the terms of the contract to each applicant—thereby making a profit out of the so-called "revolvers"—borrowers who do not pay their balance in full from month to month, but who do not ultimately default.[20] As a result, it became possible to lend to more people. But that is not all. Starting in the 1960s, as we have seen, aspiring capitalists in MBA programs were no longer taught to consider the individual security in terms of the expected return alone, but were instead taught to consider what a given security contributes to an overall portfolio, in terms of both expected return and risk. What this means, in the present context, is that Moneybags became less concerned with determining which individuals he might choose to lend to (or the particular companies in which he might invest) than with trying to construct and maintain an overall portfolio of assets—a portfolio the content of which he would constantly modify in order to achieve a desired rate of risk and return.[21]

In this context, then—and this is key—the credit score (and associated measures) not only became useful in determining the probability of default among prospective borrowers, it could also be used to determine the lender's overall exposure from having made specific loans. In effect, once it became possible for lenders to evaluate the risk associated with holding specific financial assets, it became possible also to evaluate the risk associated with a portfolio of assets. And this in turn can help us understand the dramatic expansion of securitization—the peculiar mechanism whereby a lender is not only able to lay claim to future value, but also, merely by virtue of holding a portfolio of securities, to borrow money on the financial markets more cheaply than she has lent it. Similar processes, incidentally, could be described wherever quantitative measures of risk have been widely adopted (for example, in today's equity markets, where individual securities are evaluated not only according to their so-called "fundamental value," but according to their volatility relative to the overall market), but for present purposes—and for the sake of illustration—let us simply consider the peculiar ways in which the rise of credit scoring contributed to the extraordinary rise of so-called "mortgage-backed securities" in the United States.

MORTGAGE-BACKED SECURITIES,
OR THE WONDERS OF DIVERSIFICATION

For years, if he was approached by an individual who wanted to buy a house, Moneybags would generally be hesitant.[22] After all, a house costs a lot of money. It can take decades for people to pay back their mortgage, and having to lend them money over such a long horizon would be enough to make any banker a little nervous. As a result, in part, home ownership in the United States was for a long time a privilege of the few—those who had sufficient resources to buy a house without the help of a bank. Starting in the 1930s, however, the U.S. federal government had the idea that it wanted to encourage home ownership. Or to put it more accurately, perhaps, it decided to encourage a certain kind of debt, on the assumption—in part—that workers who have a mortgage to pay are less likely than others to go on strike.[23] To that end, it resolved to facilitate lending by private banks: first by offering insurance to mortgage lenders (through the Federal Housing Administration and the Federal National Mortgage Association, established in 1935 and 1938, respectively) and then by developing a secondary market for mortgages.[24]

If Moneybags knew that he could find someone else to buy the debt before it came to maturity, the reasoning went, perhaps he might be more inclined to make the loan in the first place. And so the government established the Federal Home Loan Mortgage Corporation (Freddie Mac) in the 1970s with the hope that it could "attract private capital for public purpose" by serving as a liaison of sorts between prospective home owners, on the one hand—who were hoping to borrow money in the primary markets—and prospective investors, on the other hand—who were looking for investment opportunities in the secondary markets.[25] The strategy was simple: Freddie Mac would buy mortgages and either hold them to maturity or resell them as mortgage-backed securities, thereby reducing the risks to lenders.

The principle was straightforward enough, but setting up a secondary market was no easy task—if only because it required that prospective buyers and sellers be able to recognize and agree on the relative quality of the goods being exchanged. As Martha Poon puts it, it was thus necessary that these mortgage debts be "converted into mobile and transferable goods whose qualities buyers and sellers [could] come to agree upon in the present, even though these qualities [would] only be expressed in the future."[26] And while in other markets there existed rating agencies such as Standard & Poor's, Fitch, or Moody's that could plausibly assess the qualities of bonds, the task of assessing the value of mortgages—not to mention the value of pools of mortgages—was arguably a more formidable one.[27] In 1995, however, the government-sponsored enterprise Freddie Mac had the idea—an idea that would eventually prove very consequential—to replace its rule-based system with a system that incorporated individuals' FICO scores in determining their mortgage risk. The FICO score had been originally based on individuals' consumer credit, of course, but this seemed as good a proxy as any for measuring how reliable an individual would be in making his or her mortgage payments, as well.

A key consequence of this decision was that it became readily possible to assess the risk associated not only with individual mortgages, but with pools of mortgages. Prior to that, as Poon explains, the risk of each individual loan was described through a set of "tools, metrics, and vocabulary" that were entirely separate from those used to describe "a securitized pool of loans as a composite whole."[28] But once the underwriting process was automated and started to incorporate FICO scores, it became possible to speak of risk in uniform terms, across platforms and over different stages of the securitization process. As Poon describes it, "score-supported statistically based underwriting programs began to flow into and merge with the rating phase of securitization."[29] For the first time, by virtue of sharing the same metrics for quantifying risk, "the primary and secondary markets were to be placed on the same calculative platform," and this, in turn, meant that Freddie Mac could issue securities of its own, the value of which could be agreed upon.[30]

In retrospect, then, it appears that once it became possible to measure the probability of individual borrowers' default, it quickly became possible to determine the risk associated with a pool of debts. As a result, it also became possible to determine the lender's own probability as a borrower, which in turn allowed her to realize—as a borrower—the benefits of having assembled a diversified portfolio. When a lender issues mortgage-backed securities, after all, she is only making promises of her own, promises that are effectively backed by the borrowers whose debts she holds. But her promises, somehow, are deemed more credible than those of many of her borrowers, and this for the simple reason that she can point to the carefully diversified nature of her portfolio. And thus, sure enough, Moneybags can not only borrow money on financial markets, but lend it anew, potentially repeating the process ad infinitum.

The basic principle behind this, admittedly, is nothing new. It has long been known—at least intuitively—that a pool of assets is in some fashion safer than a single asset, and when Shylock calls Antonio a "good man," it is not because he thinks he has a good soul; it is simply that he knows him to have three ships.[31] But while this understanding of diversification may have made Shylock a discriminating lender, it could not help him determine precisely how much to lend Antonio, and it certainly could not have helped him securitize the debt, even if he had so desired. For all his cunning, Shylock had no way of systematically comparing Antonio with other prospective borrowers or of establishing his own creditworthiness, and that may be why Shylock ultimately could speak only in the moralizing language of his day—calling Antonio a good man (without specifying how good) even if, deep down, he surely cared very little about his character. By the end of the twentieth century, however, it was not only possible for lenders to calculate the likelihood of individuals defaulting on their debt, it was even possible for them to imagine that they could calculate the probability of several borrowers defaulting at the same time (thanks to the development of what is known as the Gaussian copula).[32] And because Moneybags could now quantify his own probability of default, he was in a position to issue promissory notes of his own—and thereby to realize the benefits of having a diversified portfolio.[33]

FINDING SAFETY IN NUMBERS

It is hard not to think, at this point, that Moneybags really has all the luck. In the nineteenth century, he had discovered the wondrous commodity that is labor power. By the late twentieth century, he could still count on labor power being readily available on the market, even if sometimes he had to go further afield, or found that labor per se has taken something like an "immaterial" form. But in addition to this, he now seems to have struck gold once again, as if there existed a new commodity, alongside labor power, that displays some of the same magical attributes.[34] The nature of the commodity is different, to be sure, but the laws governing its exchange are much the same. Indeed, just as workers in Marx's account were paid only what they needed to reproduce themselves as workers (and just as this exchange was construed as fair according to the law of value), in recent years, a similar arithmetic and a similar ethic have come to surround the allocation of credit. As individual borrowers, we are told, the credit we receive is merely a function of our credit score—which, in turn, is but an expression of our probability of default. In other words, the specific terms of the loans we receive are merely a function of the risk associated with holding our debts, and the loans themselves—in principle—should neither strengthen nor weaken our hand or that of our lenders. The conceit, in fact, is that we merely get the credit we deserve—or more precisely, the credit we need to reproduce ourselves as borrowers with a given level of risk: nothing more, nothing less. And yet, however equitable and fair the terms of this contract may appear, it is also clear that the creditor finds himself in a position not only to extract interest from his debtors, but also to borrow (and bet) more money than he has lent—as if somehow by appropriating other people's promise-making abilities, he had become more credible himself.

How is this possible? The ruse is the same as ever. Indeed, when Moneybags goes to market today, we may assume that what he finds are really the same vulnerable individuals as before. Only this time, the individuals he encounters are not simply free and forced to alienate their labor power. To the precise extent that they have property in their own person, they are also free (and, increasingly, forced) to speak in their own name and to decide on their own future. These are liberal subjects, after all—*neoliberal* subjects, in fact, who are both expected and encouraged to make their own choices.[35] They are individuals who have "the right to make promises" (as per Friedrich Nietzsche's formulation), but who have increasingly little choice but to do so—that is, who are to varying degrees compelled by necessity to make promises and thereby make their probability available to others for gambling purposes. Whether it be the corporate person who must issue bonds in order to raise capital or the ordinary consumer who must use a credit card in order to shop online, the individual Moneybags encounters on today's financial markets is an individual—like him—whose world is increasingly saturated with risk—an individual, indeed, who is not only in pursuit of money, but in pursuit of credit, if she is to reproduce herself successfully as a borrower or as an investor.

What does Moneybags receive in exchange for this credit? Concretely, not very much: a promise of repayment, a person's word. But Moneybags has read enough J. L. Austin to know that it is possible to do some things with words, and presumably that is why for so many years he took such care to verify that his borrowers were "serious"—that they were not joking or reciting poems, which would have meant that their promises were "hollow or void" or otherwise not felicitous.[36] And as we have seen, Moneybags has also read Markowitz, and maybe even some Jacques Derrida. As a result, by the end of the twentieth century, Moneybags seems no longer to care whether or not a promise will be kept (or, to put it in the language of French philosophy, whether or not a letter will reach its destination), so long as he thinks he can calculate the probability that the promise will be kept or that some letters will arrive. Moneybags no longer needs to concern himself with whether an applicant is or is not credible (or whether a company will be profitable in the long run), provided that he can estimate just how credible he is at any moment—or more precisely, how likely it is that he will make good on his payments. This seems to suffice, for Moneybags now has at his disposal an entire portfolio of letters and all the computing power and elegance of modern mathematical finance, which together allow him to arrange his portfolio just so while at the same time concealing—to a large extent—the dense social relations and the peculiar kind of violence that are required for such a portfolio to exist in the first place.

Moneybags knows how lucky he is. Already in the nineteenth century, he could be heard laughing to himself, for he knew what awaited the laborer in the workshop.[37] There, in "the hidden abode of production," he knew that the laborer would find equipment and materials,

> Every condition of the problem is satisfied, while the laws governing the exchange of commodities have not been violated in any way. Equivalent has been exchanged for equivalent. For the capitalist as buyer paid the full value for each commodity, for the cotton, for the spindle and for the labour-power. He then did what is done by every purchaser of commodities: he consumed their use-value. (Marx, *Capital*, vol. 1, pp. 301–302)

products of labor that Moneybags had bought earlier that week, also at their value.[38] All day long, the laborer would mix his labor power with these spindles and this cotton, and in so doing, he would create more products, more value than he himself would need to reproduce himself as laborer. As for Moneybags, he had simply to sell these products, and in doing so, he would realize, as profit, all the surplus value created by the laborer. Moneybags was laughing, in other words, because he knew that however fair the exchange between the employer and employee appeared, it was he, the capitalist, who controlled the means of production and was therefore able to command the labor power of the worker and render it productive of value.

Today, Moneybags is laughing still, and I imagine it is for much the same reasons as before. He knows, for one thing, that while a corporate bond or a credit card receipt may not contain much labor power in and of itself, it does represent a claim on future value (it is what Marx called "fictitious capital").[39] But that is not the only reason for Moneybags's laughter; Moneybags knows also that when a corporation issues a bond or a consumer swipes a credit card, they are mixing something of themselves in these paper bonds and credit card receipts — something of their credibility that can be of use to him.[40] After all, if, in the nineteenth century, the worker's labor power could be mixed with the dead labor of others, couldn't the same now be done with his promises? And indeed, when Moneybags at the end of the day gathers the promissory notes of home owners, it is with the understanding that these have already been combined with the promises of countless others: other borrowers whose credit history and credit scores are already embedded or congealed in the various data, microprocessors, and algorithms that Moneybags so secretly guards. It is because these assets are combined, in other words, that Moneybags is able to achieve such extraordinary results — much as it was by bringing workers together in the same plant that the factory owner was able to "put them to work."

The key players in financial markets today, it should be noted, are rarely individuals trading for their own account so much as their delegates—such as the mutual-fund, pension-fund, or hedge-fund managers who, by combining one person's savings with the savings of myriad others, are able to develop portfolios that are more efficient than what individual investors could have achieved on their own.[41] The power of JPMorgan, Goldman Sachs, or their earthly representatives, in other words (or the extraordinary power of the rating agencies, which our figure of Moneybags unfortunately elides), comes less from the money they have to their name (though that may be what their power results in) than from their control over what Marx called the means of production—which could also be described, in this instance, as the means of *prediction*.[42] As Markowitz himself points out, in fact, one of the ways that modern portfolio theory differs from earlier theories of investment is that it can be "used to direct practice, at least by large (usually institutional) investors with sufficient computer and database resources."[43] And it is this control over the means of prediction, it would seem, that allows some individuals to make use of the capabilities and probabilities of others in such a fashion that they become more capable and probable in turn. They do this, of course, while remaining both within the bounds of liberal contract law and under the blinding light of modern probability theory, the formalism of which provides them with added legitimacy, since the mathematical principles at work (for example, the principle of diversification) appear as unassailable truths, eclipsing the fact that much as workers had to be brought together on the factory floor in order for their labor power to become productive of value, someone must hold a portfolio in order for the virtues of diversification to become manifest.[44]

CONCLUSION

When Marx undertook his landmark critique of political economy a hundred and fifty years ago, he began not in the realm of production, as might have been expected, but in the realm of circulation. There, he explained, we may think of ourselves as equal partners in a free and fair exchange, and we may think of the objects we exchange as merely that: objects to be exchanged. But even this fiction cannot entirely conceal the fact that these objects first have to be made—produced by human hands—before they can be traded. And when Marx invited us into the hidden abode of production to consider not only how these commodities are made, but how value itself is produced, we began to take the measure of what is both hidden and presupposed by the idyllic stories of bourgeois economics. In particular, we began to take the measure of what it means for relations of production themselves to be mediated by money and for labor—or more precisely, labor power—to be treated as a "thing," a commodity like any other, the cost of which can be written down on a ledger just as easily as the cost of fertilizer or heavy machinery.

In precapitalist societies, as Anselm Jappe reminds us, it would not have occurred to anyone to put on the same level as abstract labor such diverse activities as "baking a loaf of bread, playing a piece of music, directing a military campaign, discovering a geometric figure or preparing a meal."[45] These were not only distinct as concrete, purposive activities, they were also embedded in particular social relations in which exploitation or domination were clearly extrinsic to the labor process. By the time of Marx's writing, however, this was no longer the case: the wage relation had become all but generalized, and labor itself was increasingly recognized as productive of value. And as money was becoming the dominant form of social mediation (according to Marx, at least), it became increasingly possible in principle not only to measure the contribution of individual workers to the production process, but to set their wages accordingly, thereby allowing the seemingly impartial but ruthless mechanism of the "market" to enforce the exacting demands of capitalist accumulation.

To this day, undoubtedly, labor remains very much a "thing," and one that continues to organize both the production and distribution of wealth where the capitalist mode of production prevails. But as we have discovered by following Moneybags back into his lair, the specific terms mediating this production process have changed in recent decades, and the categories on the capitalist's ledger have multiplied. A factory manager at General Motors, presumably, will still be looking for ways to increase profitability and putting pressure on her workers accordingly, but she will likely have some new concerns, as well. Indeed, though she may still want productivity to reach an all-time high, she knows also that her company's market valuation—and hence her own livelihood—will depend at least as much on the company's *imagined* prospects as on any measure of its actual performance.

As for her colleagues at Ally Financial Inc., or what used to be known as the General Motors Acceptance Corporation (GMAC), they, too, are surely trying to achieve maximum profits for their parent company. But in their case, this likely means they are concerned with increasing yield and minimizing risk or with assessing the rate of default among their borrowers and adjusting their rates accordingly. Happily for them, they have techniques and strategies at their disposal, and just as it is second nature for the factory foreman to count the number of hours worked and the number of cars produced, it is likewise second nature for the loan officer or the risk manager to consider an applicant's credit history before agreeing to a loan.

Of course, it should be noted that the good people at Ally Financial are workers in their own right, whose individual contribution to their company's profit margin is surely being evaluated and rewarded with an appropriate wage or bonus (or so one should hope: in 2004, GMAC— with earnings of $2.9 billion—accounted for 80 percent of GM's net income).[46] But that is not the point. The point, rather, is that all of these workers—whether in Ally Financial's risk management department or on the assembly line of GM's remaining factories—may be just as vulnerable to changes in the annual percentage rate (APR) on their automobile loan as they are to changes in the terms of their employment contract proper. And as if to complicate matters further, these workers may even find in their later years that it is the ups and downs of the stock market that concern them the most, since it is the success or failure of their pension plan that will determine their share of the global surplus—a surplus to which they will themselves have contributed by their past labors.

In the century and a half since the publication of *Capital*, for better or for worse, Marx has been widely celebrated (or denounced) for having offered a critique of society from the standpoint of labor. And perhaps he did. But it may be more accurate—or more helpful, at any rate—to acknowledge the ways in which Marx's critique is first and foremost a critique *of* labor, as Moishe Postone puts it, or more generally a critique of modern society and its historically specific forms of social mediation. On such a reading, Marx's great merit lies not in having identified labor as the true and rightful source of wealth, nor is it simply that he described the brutality of laborers' working conditions. Rather, his greatest contribution may be to have called our attention to what forms of domination and exploitation are made possible and concealed, what relations are legitimated and disavowed, when a society is so committed to the pursuit and accumulation of value that it treats labor as a thing—a thing that can be measured, abstracted, exchanged. If the foregoing analysis has any merit, likewise, it lies not in having identified some new source of value (which it has not), or in having explained the extraordinary expansion of financial markets (though it may have, at least in part). The narrative, after all, has hewed too closely to Marx's own to yield anything really new. But while it may be that the pursuit of profit is a defining constant in the history of capitalism, the precise forms of exploitation and predation that it produces are not. And if the terms of these relations evolve, undoubtedly, the terms of their critique must change, as well.[47]

CHAPTER FOUR

From Vagabond to Subprime:
The Making of *Homo probabilis*

Toward the end of *Capital*'s first volume, most of which proceeds—
however ironically—within the idiom of classical political economy,
Marx finally changes registers and distances himself explicitly from
the bourgeois economists whose work he has been critiquing all
along.[1] In particular, Marx takes a swipe at those economists who
seem to treat the existence of the "free worker" and his confronta-
tion with the capitalist as an eternal and natural fact, or, as per Adam
Smith's formulation, as the result of some "previous process of accumulation" now long forgotten.[2] As Marx puts it with his usual verve,
this "primitive accumulation plays approximately the same role in
political economy as original sin does in theology. Adam bit the apple,
and thereupon sin fell on the human race."[3] The origin of this sin,
Marx goes on to say, "is supposed to be explained when it is told as an
anecdote about the past. Long, long ago there were two sorts of people;
one, the diligent, intelligent and above all frugal élite; the other, lazy
rascals, spending their substance, and more, in riotous living.... Thus
it came to pass that the former accumulated wealth, and the latter sort
finally had nothing to sell except their own skins."[4]

Against this naively benign (if thoroughly ideological) account of
how the division of society into two classes came to be—an account
that, he seems to imply, serves only to legitimate the continued exploitation of workers by capitalists—Marx offers in the book's final

chapters a fuller account of the violent processes through which this "so-called primitive accumulation" in fact occurred.[5] "In actual history," writes Marx, "it is a notorious fact that conquest, enslavement, robbery, murder, in short, force, play the greatest part."[6] First, starting in the fifteenth century, through a series of both illegal and legal means, peasants were dispossessed of the land to which they had previously had access. Coupled with the dissolution of bands of feudal retainers, this expropriation of the peasants gave rise to a "free and rightless proletariat" that "could not possibly be absorbed by the nascent manufactures as fast as it was thrown upon the world."[7] The result was that people were turned "in massive quantities into beggars, robbers and vagabonds" who all but flooded the nascent towns of Western Europe.[8] There, as Marx puts it, a "bloody legislation" was put in place "at the end of the fifteenth and during the whole of the sixteenth centuries" that sought to criminalize vagabondage and that eventually made possible the creation of a new industrial working class—or more precisely perhaps, the creation of a new kind of population: a population of *individuals*, who may have had property in their own person and who were thus free to demand a wage in exchange for their labors, but who, by dint of having no other claim to property, had little choice but to submit freely to the exigencies of industrial capital.

Looking back on the history of capitalism since the time of Marx's writing, it is hard not to be struck by the fact that the violence that Marx so vividly described—a violence that Marx seemed to think belonged squarely to the prehistory of capital—has in fact been part and parcel of its entire history. As David Harvey has argued, it may be more helpful to speak no longer of a "primitive accumulation," lest one think of it as a process that has been completed once and for all, but instead of an "accumulation by dispossession"—a process that is clearly unfolding to this day, wherever noncapitalist societies are being brought into the fold or wherever there is a "deepening" of advanced capitalism at the expense of "traditional" forms of capitalism.[9] As

Saskia Sassen documents, indeed, such a process can just as easily be found in developing countries that have been ravaged by years of debt-servicing regimes as in the United States where financial innovations over the last twenty years have resulted in the destruction of millions of households and have led to the "expulsion" of people from their traditional "capitalist encasements."[10]

In the following pages, I, too, make a case for returning to Marx's analysis of early modern Europe as a way to help us understand our own predicament, but I do so with a slightly different emphasis and set of concerns. Specifically, where Harvey, Sassen, and others have found in Marx's analysis of "primitive accumulation" a way to underscore the remarkable continuities in the history of capitalism—and in particular, the relentless violence that capitalism seems to visit upon the most vulnerable populations—my aim in the present chapter is chiefly to reflect on the *discontinuous* nature of contemporary capitalism. More specifically yet, if I turn in the following pages to Marx's analysis of capitalism's emergence, it is with an eye to what it might teach us about the transformation of Anglo-American capitalism in the last forty years—a transformation characterized by the dramatic rise of the financial sector and the concurrent emergence of the recognizably neoliberal subject and set of relations that are defining attributes of what I have termed today's portfolio society.

The argument of this chapter, simply put, is that advanced capitalist societies have undergone changes in recent decades that are in many ways analogous to those undergone by European societies some five hundred years ago. At the time, as we have already seen, the sudden enclosure of the commons in England created a population that had little choice but to flee the countryside in order to survive. As they moved to the cities, these expropriated peasants were met with extraordinarily harsh laws against vagabondage, and as a result, there emerged over the years a new population of individuals suitably disciplined for the rigors of factory work and the industrial labor market. Likewise, in recent decades, as I will argue in the first part of the chapter, the end of Keynesianism and the demise of the welfare state in both Europe and the United States have had similarly dislocating effects, confronting people with a form of insecurity against which they had previously been shielded—or more precisely, a form of insecurity against which they had previously shielded each other collectively. Many people have become vagabonds as a result of this, and much as in the sixteenth century, their poverty has often been criminalized. But more remarkably, perhaps, a great many of them have been forced to seek alternative forms of protection—if not in the cities per se, as in the story that Marx tells, then in the world of finance, or to put it differently, in the City itself, as Londoners like to call their financial district. Thus, for instance, the collapse of the Bretton Woods monetary regime had the effect that many companies and countries that once relied on the stability of a fixed exchange rate turned to the nascent derivatives markets to manage their newly discovered risks. Similarly, when employers in the United States ceased to contribute to pension plans or to offer health insurance to their employees, millions of American workers found themselves having to face the risks of old age and ill health not as a community, but as individuals, through the use of their pension funds or through private health insurance plans. The result, we already know, has been an extraordinary expansion of the financial sector and of financial markets.[11] But what kind of larger social transformation does this represent? What kind of new relations does it augur? And does it not result ultimately in an increased vulnerability to risk, since these actors are now at the mercy of a fickle and unpredictable stock market, the growth of which is as imperative as it is uncertain?

As I will further argue in the latter part of this chapter, one way of describing the financialization of Anglo-American capitalism is as having entailed not only the erosion of formerly mutualized relations of risk and protection, but also as an enclosure of the market itself—an enclosure that is inseparable from the emergence of a distinctly neo-liberal order in which people are not simply disciplined as individuals capable of alienating their labor power in exchange for a wage, but are also constructed as individuals and populations (indeed, as "dividuals," as others have aptly pointed out) whose credibility or probability can similarly be measured, abstracted, and exchanged.[12] In other words, much as the capitalism of yore required the production and reproduction of a liberal, laboring subject—one whose capacity to work could not only be measured, but also bought or sold—today's financialized capitalism and associated mode of prediction would seem to be similarly dependent on the existence of a *probable* man—a *Homo probabilis*, that is, one who can both count and be counted upon.[13]

THE GOLDEN AGE OF ACTUALLY EXISTING CAPITALISM

Our story begins not in the fifteenth or sixteenth century, but in the latter half of the twentieth, at a time when in countries such as Britain, France, or the United States, at least, life was not without its charms or without a certain form of solidarity—at least for a certain subset of the population. The working class was still exploited by capital, to be sure, but for the most part, the conditions that Marx had described in the 1860s no longer obtained. Already by the end of the nineteenth century, in fact, partly because of the ruthlessness of these conditions and partly because of Marx's own "ruthless criticism" thereof, the market society that been constructed in the eighteenth century had become largely discredited.[14] As Karl Polanyi explains, the effects of laissez-faire on the population had been so devastating—and the crises it created so severe—that measures were devised to shield those most vulnerable from the vagaries of the market.[15] In France, Britain, and Germany, the late nineteenth and early twentieth centuries saw the establishment of something like a social state, and by the 1930s, even the United States could be seen to reconsider its commitment to the "free market" that had defined the period of the Roaring Twenties. By the middle of the century, most of the national economies of Western Europe and the United States had been significantly reorganized around political compromises between formerly competing actors, and the basic schemes that had once protected the indigent had been transformed into full-blown "welfare states."[16]

To put it schematically, the bargain went something like this, at least on the national level: workers agreed not to strike, and capital, in exchange, conceded a larger share of its profits than before—not only through better wages and through more secure long-term employment contracts, but also through a variety of new benefits: health, retirement, and unemployment insurance, access to free public education, and so on. This allowed workers to enjoy higher living standards while simultaneously ensuring that capitalists would find a broad consumer base. But most significantly, perhaps, it meant that people in what is now called the Global North were spared from having to go through the market to meet their every need. They benefited instead from the existence of a commons of sorts, meaning that life in the welfare state had largely been "decommodified," as Gøsta Esping-Andersen has put it, and that the *société ouvrière* of the nineteenth century (as Robert Castel called it in his account of nineteenth-century France) had largely transitioned into a *société salariale*, or "wage-earning society."[17] Workers were no longer living and working under conditions of utter precarity. Instead, their condition as salaried workers afforded them a modicum of security and protection that allowed them to look beyond their next paycheck and build a better future for themselves and their communities. And when the next paycheck did arrive, they also knew they could deposit it in a bank that was both regulated and insured: even in the United States, after all, the Great Crash of 1929 had persuaded the government to establish the Federal Deposit Insurance Corporation (FDIC) and to prevent commercial banks from speculating on the stock market.

On a global level, too, the postwar years were characterized by something of a grand bargain among formerly warring countries. Indeed, to the extent that life in advanced capitalist societies did in fact correspond to the idyllic portrait I have just sketched (and for the most part, it admittedly did not, save perhaps for a privileged minority of white men with "traditional" families), it was not simply thanks to the domestic political bargains brokered by the state between capital and labor.[18] To a significant extent, the arrangements just described—as well as the Keynesian policies that accompanied them—were themselves predicated on an international arrangement that had been devised toward the end of the Second World War, also under the influence of John Maynard Keynes. It was Keynes, after all, who—together with Harry Dexter White—had helped devise the Bretton Woods monetary system: a system of fixed exchange rates in which the United States (which by then held nearly 80 percent of the world's gold reserves) not only agreed to the convertibility of other currencies into dollars, but agreed to the convertibility of dollars into gold at a fixed exchange rate of $35 per ounce.[19] This was a system, as Geoff Mann puts it, in which capitalist monies could be freely exchanged without any need for frantic trading, in large part because the currencies and the corresponding economies also had the "backstop" of the World Bank and International Monetary Fund—two institutions that had also been established at the end of the war to help in the reconstruction and transformation of those economies that had been most devastated by the conflict.[20] There, too, of course, it was the richer countries—especially the United States—that contributed disproportionately. But there, too, the United States was willing to foot a larger share of the bill, if only because the arrangement would help create stable trading relationships and a potential market for U.S. goods. By midcentury, in retrospect, something of a new "commons" thus had been established on both a national and an international level, in the sense that individuals and communities (of a certain type, again) were in principle able to partake in all aspects of capitalist production and exchange with the confidence that while the means of production may have been privately held, the system of exchange on which capitalism depended was itself available to all.

By the early 1970s, as is now well known, the political basis for both the international monetary system and the national welfare states of many advanced capitalist economies began to fray as the United States found itself increasingly unable (or unwilling) to meet the global demand for gold, leading Richard Nixon in 1971 to suspend the convertibility of dollars into gold. On one level, the policy change proved remarkably successful, if only because it exported inflation and spread the cost of the war in Vietnam around the world.[21] The more lasting consequence of the decision, however, lay in the dismantling of the system of mutualizing of risks that had characterized the Bretton Woods system, which in turn had the effect of introducing—or reintroducing—an element of uncertainty in economic life that had not existed since 1944. Without the anchor provided by the dollar's convertibility to gold, countries and companies that had been involved in international trade were now confronted with the uncertainties and risks associated with fluctuating exchange rates—risks that they would very quickly have to learn to manage by turning to the newly burgeoning markets in financial derivatives.[22]

Domestically, too, the compromise between labor and capital was becoming strained. Starting in the 1960s and 1970s, labor had become strong enough that when growth started to slow, capital found itself unable to reduce labor costs without cutting into profits and thus grew increasingly frustrated. As David Harvey would put it, capital had encountered a limit, and it was not until the late 1970s—in 1979, to be precise—that it found a way circumvent it.[23] In October of that year, then-chairman of the U.S. Federal Reserve Paul Volcker resolved to allow interest rates to rise in the hopes that this would break the back of inflation. The strategy worked: from 1980 to 1983, inflation dropped from 13 to 3 percent, but the true significance of the "Volcker shock" extended well beyond the immediate reduction of inflation: not only did the shock dramatically increase the size and importance of bond markets, it also sounded the death knell for Keynesian policy making and for the societal bargain that had underpinned it.[24]

THE "GREAT RISK SHIFT" AND THE RISE OF FINANCE

In the years that followed, thanks in large part to the work of Margaret Thatcher and Ronald Reagan, the mutualizing of risk on which the so-called "Golden Age" of capitalism depended—and which it simultaneously made possible—was largely undone as the capitalist class

> The history of this expropriation assumes different aspects in different countries, and runs through its various phases in different orders of succession, and at different historical epochs. Only in England, which we therefore take as our example, has it the classic form. (Marx, *Capital*, vol. 1, p. 876)

was allowed to disengage from the commitments to which it had been bound for the previous thirty years, and as Depression-era banking regulations were rewritten to allow a dramatic reconfiguration of the world's financial markets.[25]

Taking the case of the United States as our exemplar, it is easy to see that as employers in the 1980s and 1990s decided that they wanted "out of the social contract" (as Jacob Hacker nicely puts it), a process was set in motion whereby risk was quickly shifted "back onto workers and their families."[26] Or to put it slightly differently, a process was set in motion whereby the means of social protection that had been held in common were suddenly enclosed, with the effect that populations that had formerly been cared for now had to seek alternative forms of protection—whether in the world of insurance or that of finance more generally.[27] And as we have already begun to see, this process of enclo-sure has required the fashioning of individuals who are not only free to "invest in their own future"or to make promises in their own name, but are increasingly compelled to do so if they are to survive as func-tioning members of the portfolio society.[28]

To wit: after the passage of Medicare and Medicaid in 1965, as Hacker explains, the share of the U.S. population with some form of health insurance reached up to 90 percent.[29] This coverage was for the most part arranged through private insurers and private medical-care providers (in Europe, it might have been provided by and through the state), but it was nonetheless among the basic benefits that came with being gainfully employed. Since the 1970s, however, employers have increasingly given up on providing this benefit. Insurance companies have been more than happy to pick up the slack, of course, but since employers are no longer willing to engage in the practice of broad risk pooling, it is the individual employees who are left to negotiate con-tracts more or less on their own—choosing among plans that may seem tailored to their needs, but are most importantly tailored to their individual risk profile. (More accurately, I should say, it is as individu-als more generally that people are now left to negotiate these contracts, which in turn means not only that they are at a marked disadvantage vis-à-vis their insurers, but that they have little choice but to fashion themselves *as* individuals—individuals whose risk profile, like their credit rating, it is increasingly their responsibility to manage.)[30]

The story is much the same in the case of old-age insurance—or what most of us, perhaps naively, still call "retirement" or "social security." In 1980, over 80 percent of medium and large firms provided their employ-ees with "defined benefit" pension plans (by 2003, Hacker notes, the share is less than a third).[31] The pension would often be modest, but it had the advantage of being fairly certain, and unlike the pension funds or 401(k) plans that would eventually take their place, defined benefit programs depended neither on the employees' individual contributions (since the contributions were made by the employer) nor on the ups and downs of the stock market.[32] Indeed, these pension schemes in many ways served to protect people from the vagaries of the stock market until a change in the U.S. tax code allowed for a shift away from defined benefit to defined contributions.[33] Today, rare is the employer who provides the kind of retirement benefits that Ford once provided its employees at the River Rouge plant, but it is not unusual for Walmart employees to have access to a 401(k)—allowing them to invest a share of their modest wages in a newly liberalized financial market. Admittedly, this gives them a chance to reap a share of the surplus in the form of a deferred income, but to the extent that it is deferred income, this only leaves them more vulnerable to both the vagaries of the market and the political pressures of the dominant class.[34]

Last, but not least, as U.S. workers have seen their wages decline and their jobs become more precarious since the 1980s, they have also found it easier than ever to apply for and obtain credit. As was already noted in an earlier chapter, no sooner did capital succeed in dismantling the labor unions than it realized it had also succeeded—however inadvertently—in destroying its own consumer base.[35] Credit was thus extended to workers whose purchasing power had been severely weakened, such that while it was becoming more and more difficult for workers to find employers willing to offer them long-term contracts, it was increasingly easy for them to find lenders who were interested in a lasting relationship. Indeed, lenders were even eager to provide people with so-called "revolving credit"—that is, lines of credit that could last indefinitely, provided the borrower was willing and able to make a small minimum payment every month.

THE BLOODLESS LEGISLATION AGAINST THE EXPROPRIATED

If we were to recast the story we have told so far strictly in terms that Marx himself might have recognized, we might say that where the late nineteenth and early twentieth centuries saw the establishment of a new kind of "commons" as social insurance schemes were developed, as banking regulations were put in place, and as life in capitalist societies was generally decommodified, the late twentieth and early

> Hence at the end of the fifteenth and during the whole of the sixteenth centuries, a bloody legislation against vagabondage was enforced throughout Western Europe. The fathers of the present working class were chastised for their enforced transformation into vagabonds and paupers. Legislation treated them as 'voluntary' criminals, and assumed that it was entirely within their powers to go on working *under the old conditions which in fact no longer existed.* (*Marx, Capital*, vol. 1, p. 896)

twenty-first centuries witnessed its dramatic "enclosure" — not only in the sense that this commons was simply privatized (though in many cases it was), but in the sense that the social relations that formed its basis were systematically undone. As a result, populations of producers that had relied on the means of protection being held in common found themselves having to devise alternatives, and in particular having to turn to Wall Street or to the City of London: to its insurance companies, pension funds, and credit card providers.

But what exactly are the conditions that awaited these "free, unprotected and rightless proletarians"?[36] What hardships have they had to endure, to what forms of discipline are they now being subjected, and with what potential consequences? In the story that Marx tells, the displaced populations of Europe were met with the harshest possible laws regarding vagabondage. Those who were caught begging were branded on their back or their forehead and were enslaved, and those who sought to escape their masters were liable to be killed.[37] Surely the newcomers to the City have been more fortunate. There is no branding, no enslavement, and in many cases, they are greeted with open arms as financial services and credit cards are foisted on them without their even asking. But does this mean that violence is altogether absent or that no form of power is at work? Clearly, the rules that govern contemporary credit relations are less "bloody" than the

> James I: Anyone wandering about and begging is declared a rogue and a vagabond. Justices of the peace in Petty Sessions are authorized to have them publicly whipped and to imprison them for six months for the first offence, and two years for the second.... Incorrigible and dangerous rogues are to be branded with an R on the left shoulder and set to hard labour, and if they are caught begging again, to be executed without mercy. (Marx, *Capital*, vol. 1, pp. 898–99)

ones that were passed in early modern Europe, but are they any less crucial in the construction of today's (neoliberal) subject?[38]

Consider, for a moment, the all-too-ordinary case of a young college graduate profiled in the *New York Times* who, having just finished her studies at the University of Washington (a wise investment in her future, she no doubt thought), decided to move to New York City in search of an apartment and a job.[39] She was lucky enough to find both, but the wages she earned as a nanny proved insufficient to cover both the rent and her monthly student loan payments, which were now coming due. The loan payments alone were in the neighborhood of $1,000 a month, and so, quite sensibly, she prioritized rent. She missed a first loan payment as a result, and thirty days later, her inattention to detail was—apparently—reported to a credit bureau. Another thirty days passed without a payment, and her negligence was now becoming a problem: her credit score had been docked several points—as had that of her father, who had kindly cosigned her loan applications a few years earlier.[40] If it happens again—and it will—their scores will likely fall below 660 or 620 (if they haven't already), at which point they will be deemed subprime by the financial industry, meaning that they will either be denied credit altogether or that the terms on which they are offered credit will be so egregious that they will wish they had never applied for a loan in the first place.[41]

Unlike the branding of the vagabond that Marx so vividly describes, the branding of the subprime does not sear the flesh. As a result, it is not visible—indeed, in many cases, the subprime borrower himself may not even understand why his loan application has been denied or why the interest rates for his existing loans have shot up to unprecedented levels. In this regard, the pressures experienced by present-day borrowers whose credibility is constantly being evaluated may be closer to the pressures experienced by workers, who worry that they might be fired, than to those felt by the displaced peasants of the sixteenth century, who worried that they might be branded a slave. After all, just as the worker is likely to see her wage diminish or disappear altogether if she is deemed less productive than others, the borrower whose credit history shows him to be less "safe" than another is likely to be saddled with fines or commensurably higher interest rates—if his loan application is not purely and simply denied. In both cases, individuals are placed in competition with one another, and in both cases, the threat of being punished—while allowing them to maintain their formal freedom—nonetheless serves to discipline them into a specific kind of behavior.

That said, the mechanisms by which people are disciplined as borrowers are also markedly different from those by which they are disciplined as workers, just as the mechanisms by which people are disciplined as managers of publicly traded companies are different from those by which they are disciplined as factory owners. The worker, in principle, is paid for the work she has already accomplished—that is, for her past productivity, even if her wage is set for work yet to be done. The borrower, by contrast, is granted a credit score that reflects his estimated risk as a borrower in days to come. Admittedly, the score itself is ostensibly based on his past performance as a borrower—and in this it does resemble the wage—but what is being estimated is the future liability he poses for the lender. Moreover, whereas two workers who are equally productive should in principle receive similar wages (though the enduring "gender gap" in earnings clearly gives the lie to this particular fiction), it is quite conceivable and seemingly acceptable that two individuals who borrow the same amount and repay their debts with the exact same regularity, but differ in other regards (say, in terms of where they live, where they buy their food, or whether they buy protective pads for their furniture) should nonetheless receive different credit scores.[42] And the reason for this discrepancy, need it be said, could simply be that in these particular respects, they were deemed to belong to different populations with differing levels of credit risk.

It is clearly the case that borrowers are pitted against each other, then, as workers already are and have been for generations, but what exactly are the terms of this competition, and to what extent are we generally aware of them? I suppose it is fairly obvious—and perhaps even acceptable—that by making my credit card payments on time, I am inevitably making someone else's record look worse by comparison. It may be slightly less intuitive, however (though presumably still acceptable) that it is those other borrowers—those whose risk profile earns them an interest rate higher than mine—who are in fact insuring our lender against the possibility, however slim, that I might actually default. Officially, mind you, their higher premium is easily explained (or justified) by the fact that they do represent a higher risk to the lender, but the fact is, it is their payments—which are larger than mine—that will be used to shield the lender against the consequences of my eventual default. And finally, though I may hate to admit it, it is also quite possible that my relatively low interest rate depends less on the fact that I have proven myself true to my word or otherwise meritorious than on the fact that others who share my zip code (or my penchant for buying wild bird seeds) have made me look like a relatively safe bet.[43]

Admittedly, the peculiar system I am describing was not devised with the express purpose of exploiting whatever historical inequities characterize a given society. In the United States, at least, it is technically illegal for lenders to discriminate on the basis of ascriptive categories such as race, gender, or age, lest they be tempted to presume that a certain type of person—say, an African-American person—is less creditworthy than another. This would be acting on prejudice, and laws have been put in place to prevent it.[44] At the same time, however, so long as a lender can empirically demonstrate that a certain kind of person—or more precisely, a person who engages in a certain kind of behavior—has a higher probability of default, this lender can in all good conscience require them to pay higher interest rates than others— even if, as individuals, they themselves have never defaulted in the past. What this means, unfortunately, is that while individual lenders may not be allowed to bring their *own* prejudices to bear on a lending decision, the regulations governing the use of credit scores do little to remedy the already decisive effects of other people's prejudices, past and present.[45]

Ultimately, it is tempting to say that as techniques for credit scoring are perfected, lenders hardly even need to inquire whether an applicant is black or white to discriminate among racial groups. The material they are allowed to gather—which indirectly reflects what social conditions the applicant is living under—tells them all they need to know. The social fact that is a person's race is therefore already embedded in the terms of the lending decision. What is more, to the extent that an individual's risk profile comes to determine the terms on which they are allowed to borrow, the more "objectively" risk is measured, the more "objective" it becomes—that is, the more it comes to govern social life reflexively, most likely amplifying what social patterns already exist—but doing so under cover of scientific neutrality.[46]

PAPER OR PLASTIC AND CASH OR CREDIT?:
LIFE IN AN ENCLOSED MARKET

In much of what precedes, I have described the financialization of contemporary capitalism as if it had somehow been inflicted by external
forces onto the most vulnerable populations, rather like the enclosures
movement described by Marx. The fact is, however, that the gradual
replacement of wages by credit, like the replacement of employer-
sponsored pensions by pension funds or the gradual erosion of state-
sponsored or city-sponsored security services in favor of private
alternatives, did not take place without significant popular support.
Though many of us may now find ourselves longing for the halcyon
days of the welfare state (those of us, in particular, who may not have
taken the measure of the protections we were afforded or of the privilege they entailed), it is also undeniable that the neoliberal promise of
the 1980s and 1990s was—and for many people remains—very entic-
ing indeed. From the invention of the 401(k)—which allows individuals to plan their own retirement as they wish, contributing as little or
as much as they want, reaping the benefits of a bustling stock market
without having to rely on a bureaucratic and inefficient state to manage their future—to the proliferation of private insurance and protection schemes that allow individuals to tailor their coverage to their
specific needs and risk profiles, the 1980s and 1990s saw the development of countless new techniques and strategies for managing risk
and wealth that appealed to a population that was becoming increasingly unable (and often unwilling) to depend on their government for
assistance. But more than any other technology, it is perhaps the credit
card (already evoked in Chapter 3), with its combined promise of freedom and security, that best embodies the promise, the dangers, and
the revolutionary character of neoliberal financialization.[47]

As myriad advertising campaigns have made clear over the years,
the credit card is presented as both an instrument of freedom and a

source of security. Whether one is in a foreign country or in one so radically transformed by deregulation that it is no longer recognizable, a credit card offers its holder the promise of protection if anything should go wrong—which is no doubt why American Express reminds us to not "leave home without it." Likewise, the fact that Visa is "everywhere you want to be" allows one to move about the market freely, even if one is barely employed or living from paycheck to paycheck. But most remarkably, perhaps, the technology of the credit card empowers a person to determine when to borrow and when to pay, and in so doing, to decide for herself on the true value of things. Thus, MasterCard, most famously, allows its users to decide what things are truly worth their price and what things are not, and in this regard, undoubtedly, it is truly "priceless."

At the same time, as many cardholders have discovered, it is easy to get entangled in the mesh of this safety net provided by the credit card. The ability to borrow afforded by the card does seem often to compound people's vulnerability, leading not to greater freedom or autonomy, but to increased levels of indebtedness, and as a result, to ever-greater dependence on capital.[48] But what is less often acknowledged than the sheer increase in the level of debt is the fact that the generalization of the credit card effectively amounts to yet another new form of enclosure—an enclosure of the market itself, so to speak—the consequences of which have yet to be fully grasped or theorized.

Consider for a moment "the market" as it existed, if not in Marx's time, at least in his imagination. As Marx puts it in *Capital*, when commodities go to market, they are accompanied by their "guardians."[49] There, the guardians recognize each other as representatives of their commodities—representatives who are equal before the law, equally entitled to alienate their property and to receive property in return. Some of them may have little to their name—indeed, they may have nothing to sell other than their own labor power, while the others have an overabundance of money they are looking to invest. But formally, at least, they always encounter each other as equals.

Though he does not dwell on this, Marx does acknowledge that in such encounters, both the seller and buyer of labor power can count on the existence of a state to protect their claims to private property, just as both can count on the existence of a universal equivalent to mediate the encounter. So long as these conditions obtain, the capitalist can expect the worker to perform the tasks demanded of her, and the worker in turn can expect that she will receive a wage—however modest—in exchange for her labor power. What is more, both worker and capitalist can trust that the money they exchange—whether when the worker gets paid or when she goes to purchase the goods she herself has produced—will be recognized as such and will allow the transaction to occur.

Fast-forward from the mid-nineteenth century to the present-day United States, however, and what do we find? Today's capitalist, to be sure, still expects the worker to work and the worker, in turn, still expects to be paid, and both continue to trust that their money will be recognized on the marketplace. But much has changed in the last one hundred and fifty years, and the seemingly immediate encounter between the buyer and the seller has grown more complex. For one thing, our present-day worker will rarely be paid in cash. More likely than not, her earnings will be deposited in a bank account—which increasingly she is required to have in order merely to be hired. For another, when she leaves work and goes to the market, what is it she encounters? In recent years, especially in the United States, many transactions that once involved only cash have become mediated by credit. Whether they are paying for repairs to their car or ordering items of clothing from an online retailer, U.S. consumers are increasingly having to produce their credit card or their credit card information—which means, of course, that they have also to produce themselves as creditworthy customers—before they can even engage in the most quotidian of market transactions.

The experience of using a credit card, admittedly, will often seem less complicated than that of using cash—and in many ways, it may even seem more immediate. Whether I am using it at the local Starbucks, for instance, or using it online to replenish my stash of Nespresso capsules, the convenience of the credit card is nearly undeniable: a swipe of the card or a stroke of the keyboard and voilà, I have my fix. And yet it almost goes without saying that on close inspection, the institutional setup that enables my coffee addiction is considerably more intricate. For one thing, though I may think that it is I who paid for my coffee, the truth of the matter is that it is my bank that has purchased it on my behalf—effectively fronting me the money for a few weeks while I maintain my habit. (I need only read the small print on the paper slip the barista has handed me to be reminded that I have merely agreed to reimburse my lender "as per the terms of the cardholder agreement.")[50]

But that is not all. The merchant, too—whether it be Starbucks, Nestlé, or the owner of a franchise—may feel similarly pleased that he now has money in the bank that he can use as he wishes. Yet while that may be true, that is only because his bank (the so-called "acquiring bank") has agreed to deposit "my" money into his account and in doing so is taking a risk for which it will have to be compensated.[51] After all, what if the barista serves me an iced hazelnut macchiato in lieu of the mocha frappuccino I ordered? Or more plausibly, what if instead of the five hundred Arpeggio capsules I wanted I am mistakenly sent fifty Volluto decaffeinated capsules? Surely I would request a refund, and the bank would have to pay me back. Because of such possibilities, the merchant will likely also be charged a risk premium by his bank, lest it find itself having to return the money unexpectedly. On both sides of such an ostensibly simple transaction, in other words, both the customer and the merchant are merely borrowing money where before they seemed to be only trading commodities. Goods and services are still exchanged, and the presence of the state is still required, but, crucially, in order merely to engage in this exchange of commodities, customers and merchants now have to be evaluated as *borrowers*. The customer is evaluated for her fitness to borrow the amounts she needs to make her purchases, and the merchant is similarly evaluated for his fitness to borrow whatever amount his business generates in credit card transactions.

In sum, where only a few years ago buyers and sellers could meet at the marketplace and use a currency that was available to all, we are increasingly finding that the marketplace itself has been enclosed. One's purchasing power is no longer simply dependent on the number of bills one has in one's wallet, but is in large part dependent on one's borrowing power or one's credit—which each of us has to negotiate as an individual. And what this means, in turn, is that much as in the nineteenth century, when most people in order to survive had to present themselves before their employer as individuals whose labor power not only could be measured and abstracted, but freely alienated in exchange for a wage, today, we are further required to present ourselves as individuals whose capacity to take risks—to make promises and be generally "probable"—can similarly be measured and appropriated in exchange for a specific line of credit.[52]

CONCLUSION

If there is one lesson to be learned from this discussion, what might it be? In the nineteenth century, political economists feigned to believe that the existence of the free worker and of the wage relation between him and the capitalist was an eternal and God-given fact. Man has a natural "propensity to truck, barter, and exchange one thing for another," Adam Smith explained, and that was that.[53] Marx exposed this for the lie that it is, highlighting along the way the extraordinary violence that had made possible the emergence of these relations and that had made it possible for "labour power" to appear as a commodity in its own right, albeit a "fictitious" one, as Karl Polanyi would later observe.[54]

Today, in the United States, we are similarly encouraged to think of ourselves as natural-born choosers, rational actors with the ability and desire to make our own decisions and accept their consequences. We may each have our idiosyncratic preferences and temperaments whereby some of us are risk averse while others are risk seeking, but overall, it is understood that we all have the same capacity and right to determine what risks to take and what commitments to make. As Michel Feher puts it, the subjects who are "presupposed and targeted by neoliberalism" are "investors in their own human capital" who can thus "be conceived as the managers of a portfolio of conducts pertaining to all the aspects of their lives."[55] We have property in our own person and in our own portfolio, so to speak—just as in the time of John Locke—and this not only entitles us to alienate our own labor power, it allows us also to make promises in our own name and to alienate our credibility to anyone who might have an interest in acquiring it.

The fact is, however, that while we may still be asked to believe that such is the natural condition of mankind, nobody is really fooled. Even the apostles of neoliberalism, in fact—*especially* the apostles of neoliberalism, I should say—all but acknowledge that this neoliberal *Homo probabilis*, this "entrepreneur of the self" or this investor on which today's capitalist mode of prediction depends, does not exist in the wild: it has to be bred.[56] Or to borrow from Simone de Beauvoir, one is not born, but rather becomes an expert in risk management. But under what terms and what conditions? As I have shown in the preceding pages, just as the emergence of the liberal individual of the nineteenth century can be traced in part to the enclosure of the land that occurred two or three centuries prior, today's neoliberal individual finds his origins in another kind of enclosure movement—the enclosure of the twentieth-century welfare state and of the market itself. And just as in the story that Marx recounts, it was the threat of enslavement, followed by the threat of unemployment (or as Marx euphemistically puts it, "the silent compulsion of economic relations") that made possible the emergence of the "free worker," in the story I have told, something of the same threat still obtains: not only because the threat of unemployment still remains, or simply because debtors' prisons have returned, but most generally because, as Pierre Le Pesant de Boisguilbert once remarked, it is as easy to "ruin a poor person" as to enrich him.[57]

CHAPTER FIVE

When Goldman Broke the Law

> To prevent possible misunderstandings, let me say this. I do not by any means depict the capitalist and the landowner in rosy colours. But individuals are dealt with here only in so far as they are the personifications of economic categories, the bearers of particular class-relations and interests. My standpoint, from which the development of the economic formation of society is viewed as a process of natural history, can less than any other make the individual responsible for relations whose creature he remains, socially speaking, however much he may subjectively raise himself above them. (Marx, *Capital*, vol. 1, p. 92)

In the summer of 2013, five years after the end of the U.S. housing bubble and the resulting collapse of the world's financial markets, a former Wall Street banker stood trial in a Manhattan district courthouse. The defendant, Fabrice Tourre—whose love letters we so indelicately quoted in the opening pages of this book—was accused of having misled clients in connection with a derivative product named ABACUS 2007-AC1, linked to the performance of subprime loans. His employer, Goldman Sachs Group Inc., had also been named as a defendant in the initial lawsuit, but had successfully settled out of court for an unprecedented $550 million in July 2010.[1] Eventually, on August 1, after three years of litigation, two and a half weeks of trial, and two days of jury deliberation, the defendant was found liable on six counts of securities fraud. At thirty-four, Fabulous Fab—as he was by then widely known—was standing alone, though not quite as he had predicted, amid "these complex, highly leveraged, exotic trades": "monstruosities" that by his own admission he had created without necessarily understanding all their implications.[2] To this day, he remains the only individual to have been successfully prosecuted in such a case in connection to the financial crisis of 2008.

It would seem easy to argue—as indeed I will be arguing in the remaining pages of this book—that Tourre is something of a scapegoat in this affair, one whose sacrifice does little to right the wrongs of Wall Street and serves instead to deflect attention from the misdeeds of others far more culpable than he. After all, Tourre is hardly the main culprit in the subprime crisis of 2007–2008, and even the singling out of Goldman Sachs—whether by Senator Carl Levin ("Boy, that Timberwolf was one shitty deal!") or by *Rolling Stone*'s Matt Taibbi (of "vampire squid" fame)—seems in many ways undeserved, given how many people were involved in usurious lending practices that pushed so many others into conditions of great precarity.[3] What is more, it goes (almost) without saying that the $820,000 fine leveled against the Frenchman, even when coupled with the half-billion dollars paid by Goldman in its settlement, pales in comparison with the trillions of dollars that have been lost by U.S. households alone or with the billions of dollars in yearly bonuses that Tourre's colleagues at Goldman and elsewhere have continued to amass—not to mention with the untold amounts of public debt that have been generated around the world as governments have sought desperately to restore liquidity to the markets by making private institutions solvent again.[4]

The truth is, however, that the ABACUS trial is no mere political theater, no minor sideshow designed simply to entertain the masses while the real culprits are allowed to roam free. For better or worse, the trial of Goldman Sachs and one of its employees—whether in the courts of law or the court of public opinion—has been one of the principal ways that the people of the United States have found to come to terms with the crisis: its causes, its consequences, and more generally, the many uncomfortable truths that it revealed about the nature of capitalism in the age of financialization. And so one wonders: What was at stake in the ABACUS trial? And what, if anything, might this particular case reveal about the workings of financial markets more generally? As Marieke de Goede so pertinently puts it, what does it mean to hold a person "individually liable amid the complex human-technological assemblage of derivative valuation," and what might we learn from such a trial about "the boundary between legitimate speculation and illegitimate fraud" in the postcrisis era?[5]

The crime ostensibly committed by Tourre, as we will see, was to have misled investors in the structuring and marketing of a derivative product, thereby violating sections of the Securities Act of 1933 and the Securities Exchange Act of 1934.[6] As we will also see, however, in taking Tourre to court, the U.S. government was not merely upholding the law of the nation. More importantly, perhaps, it was also defending the law of the market. And if, in this context, Tourre can indeed be justly described as a scapegoat, it is not merely because there are others more culpable than he. It is, rather, because his trial serves—potentially—to restore a faith in the market and the purity of its laws, a faith that, for better or worse, the crisis of 2007–2008 had done much to call into doubt.

SEC V. TOURRE

The story of ABACUS, as far as the courts are concerned, begins in 2006, when a hedge fund manager named John Paulson, having monitored the evolution of the U.S. subprime market over several months, came to the conclusion that it would most likely collapse before too long. Paulson had identified a number of BBB-rated residential mortgage-backed securities (RMBSs) composed of mortgages in Arizona, California, Florida, and Nevada that he expected would experience a dramatic drop in value as more and more borrowers kept defaulting, and on the basis of this assessment, he devised a strategy that would allow him to bet against the market. The plan went something like this: What if a well-respected investment bank—say, Goldman Sachs—could create a synthetic collateralized debt obligation, a CDO, that would specifically refer to (or, in the parlance of Wall Street, "reference") some of the troubled securities that Paulson had in mind? This would allow Paulson to buy protection on specific layers of the capital structure while simultaneously letting him have a hand in the selection of the so-called reference portfolio. The deal would cost him some money to arrange, but if his calculations were right, Paulson stood to make a rather handsome profit, even in case of a market downturn.

In exchange for a small ($15 million) fee, Goldman agreed to the proposal and tasked the young Tourre with assembling the product. Tourre forwarded Paulson's proposed list of RMBSs to a third party—a company named ACA Management LLC (ACA), which had constructed and managed a number of comparable CDOs in previous years and had thus acquired some experience analyzing credit risk in residential mortgage-backed securities. ACA duly examined the proposed list of underlying securities, modified it to its liking, and soon agreed to serve as the official "portfolio selection agent" for the ABACUS CDO.[7] Only, according to the SEC, Tourre in his dealings with ACA was not entirely candid about Paulson's role—or more precisely, about his motives—in the initial selection of securities. Tourre never informed ACA of Paulson's intention to "short" the market, nor did he disabuse them of the impression that Paulson was going to be an equity investor. Finally, once the ABACUS product was fully structured, Tourre assembled the relevant marketing materials to distribute to potential investors—such as the German commercial bank IKB

Deutsche Industriebank AG (IKB) and the Dutch bank ABN AMRO. But there, too, it seems that Tourre was not entirely forthcoming: his marketing material made no mention of Paulson's role, and potential investors were thus led to believe that it was ACA alone that had chosen the reference obligations.

In light of the facts just described, the SEC came to the determination that Tourre had made "materially misleading statements and omissions"—meaning not only that he had deliberately concealed or misrepresented some facts, but that his deception had been distinctly consequential, leading individuals and institutions to behave in ways they would not have otherwise.[8] The SEC implied that Goldman's communications had led ACA to misconstrue Paulson's intentions and that—as Tourre well knew—ACA would have acted differently if they had not thought of Paulson as an equity investor. Likewise, the SEC also deemed that Tourre's presentation of ACA as sole portfolio selection agent was deliberately misleading and had persuaded IKB and ABN AMRO to invest in a product that, had Goldman Sachs been fully candid, they would have known to avoid. The ABACUS product had been deliberately designed to fail, in other words, and when indeed it did fail (by January 2008, 99 percent of the reference securities had been downgraded), the investors (the "protection sellers") in ABACUS 2007-AC1 lost over $1 billion, while Paulson reaped about the same amount in profit.

Against these charges, Goldman's and Tourre's response was disarmingly simple. Already before the trial, Tourre had told the Senate's Permanent Subcommittee on Investigations that his job between 2004 and 2007 had been "primarily to make markets for clients."[9] And this, he explained, meant that he was simply "connecting clients who wished to take a long exposure to an asset—meaning they anticipated the value of the asset would rise—with clients who wished to take a short exposure to an asset—meaning they anticipated the value of the asset would fall."[10] Tourre was only doing his job as "market maker," in other words, quoting figures to clients and allowing them to decide for themselves on the judiciousness of their potential investments. This was presumably Goldman's way of "doing God's work," as its chairman Lloyd Blankfein might have put it, or—to borrow once again from Tourre's private correspondence—Goldman's way of "mak[ing] capital markets more efficient and ultimately provid[ing] the U.S. consumer with more efficient ways to leverage and finance himself."[11]

There was undoubtedly a certain elegance to Tourre's line of reasoning. These were "sophisticated investors," after all (as Tourre and Goldman did not tire of repeating), which would suggest that they were actors who were fully capable of deciding for themselves on the worth of the securities on offer. Moreover, as Tourre also pointed out before the Senate, these were really "institutions," not individuals, by which he either meant that they were not real people anyway or, more plausibly, that with all the PhDs on their payroll, these companies could be expected to run the numbers on their own.[12] And the truth is, as was already mentioned, ACA had indeed arranged comparable deals in the past, and Tourre's 196-page "flip book" describing the ABACUS CDO certainly did include a list of the referenced securities, together with their ratings and the average remaining life spans on the actual mortgages themselves.[13]

But there's the rub. While it may be a core belief of liberal economics that markets, if left alone, will be self-regulating and ensure an optimal allocation of resources along the way, it is also understood that in practice, prices cannot be expected to quote themselves. Even the most "sophisticated" investors, it turns out, depend on other individuals and institutions, and in the market for over-the-counter derivatives, especially, the role of these intermediaries is of particular importance. As one expert witness put it, investors in a synthetic CDO rely "in the most fundamental way" on the portfolio manager and the issuing dealer, and that is why it is so crucial that these individuals be both competent and impartial—a combination of virtues for which, admittedly, they are handsomely rewarded.[14]

Goldman and Tourre knew all this, of course, but according to the SEC, they also knew that it would be "difficult, if not impossible," to "place the liabilities of a synthetic CDO" if they disclosed to potential clients that a short investor such as Paulson had "played a significant role in the collateral selection process."[15] That is presumably why Tourre was so eager to enlist ACA as selection agent and why he also sought to ensure that ACA be credited as such in the product's marketing material. Indeed, as Tourre put it a tad too candidly in an internal e-mail, "one thing that we need to make sure ACA understands is that we want their name on this transaction," for it "will be important that we can use ACA's branding to help distribute the bonds."[16]

"I FOUGHT THE LAW AND THE LAW WON"

In the end, needless to say, Tourre's private correspondence trumped his public testimony. His e-mails provided evidence of *scienter* on his part, meaning that he was aware of the wrongness of his deeds, and the jurors were thus finally convinced that his intention all along had been to deceive. But regardless of the precise reasons Tourre may have ultimately been found guilty by a jury of his peers, one may still reasonably wonder: Why exactly did Tourre stand accused of fraud in the first place? After all, the SEC is not typically concerned with policing the morals of Wall Street traders, nor is it officially tasked with protecting the interests of particular individuals and institutions. It is "first and foremost" a "law enforcement agency," as its Web site reminds us—one that is tasked with preserving the integrity of the market, the functioning of which had presumably been compromised.[17]

And here, two possibilities suggest themselves. On the one hand, it might be acknowledged that by making "materially misleading statements and omissions," Tourre was not simply doing Paulson's bidding.

He was interfering with the proper functioning of the market in general, and for this reason, he had to be prosecuted. On the other hand, it is also possible to spin the story in a slightly different way, whereby Tourre's gravest sin—or his greatest misfortune, at any rate—had less to do with the fact that he cheated than with the fact that by doing so (and by leaving a trace of his misdeeds), he had inadvertently revealed that it is always *possible* to cheat. On this reading, then, Tourre's mistake was not merely to have somehow "fixed" the game in favor of his client or thereby to have defrauded some rich investors. More importantly, it was that by his actions, he had revealed or threatened to reveal something that must always remain hidden if markets are allowed to work their magic—namely, that markets are indeed "made," and made by individuals who are inevitably embedded in unequal relations of power.

But if that is indeed the case, then our question must become: What is the nature of this market that the SEC seeks so valiantly to defend? What functions does it serve, and what value does it have? And is there not something slightly disingenuous, at the very least, about the moral outrage surrounding this case—something akin to the righteous indignation of *Casablanca*'s Captain Renault, say, when, as the German police order him to shut down Rick's café, the French officer declares himself "shocked, shocked to find out that gambling is going on here," while at the same time collecting his winnings of the night?

To put it differently: If we examine the kind of honest transactions IKB and ABN AMRO thought they were entering into when they became the clients of Goldman Sachs—or, for that matter, the kind of transactions that are carried out daily on financial markets more generally—what will we find? Will we find equitable transactions between honest partners, or will we find practices and norms that are at least as disturbing as the fraudulent deals of which Tourre stands accused? It is understandable, of course, that IKB, ACA, and ABN

AMRO should have been upset to discover that a deal they thought was fair had in fact been rigged. But were they dismayed to learn that the game had been fixed, or was it just that it had not been fixed in the way they had expected? When IKB, ABN AMRO, and ACA entered into a relationsip with Goldman and Paulson, it was with the understanding that they were among "sophisticated" investors who would not be taking advantage of each other, but were they not themselves expecting to take advantage of something or someone else? And judging from all that we have seen, did they not know, *in foro interno*, that the people whose mortgages they were betting on were people who—like them, it turns out—had been lured by the promise of a fair exchange into what was, in fact, a profoundly unequal bargain?

FAWLTY TOWERS: THE MAKING OF A CDO

It is an oft-noted fact that synthetic CDOs and credit derivatives of the type that Tourre was asked to put together are inordinately "complex," "exotic," and "sophisticated." Indeed, that is both how the media have reported on this and other cases and how these contracts are described in the idiom of quantitative finance—and often with good reason. At the same time, however, it should also be possible to describe the structure of a synthetic CDO in fairly simple terms as a kind of tower in which each level entails the securitization of the level below.[18]

At the bottom of the tower, the metaphor goes, are residential mortgages—subprime mortgages, in the case at hand, of the kind that were extended in such great quantities in the years leading up the crisis. Taken individually, these are mortgages that would be impossible for lenders to part with, given the risk associated with holding them. But once they are pooled together by a securitization sponsor (say, Goldman Sachs), they can be transferred to a "special purpose vehicle" (SPV), which has the ability to issue securities of its own and is, in the language of the trade, "bankruptcy remote."[19] These are the infamous "residential mortgage-backed securities," which form the second level of the tower.

The structure of these securities is by now well known: As borrowers send in their monthly payments, the SPV passes on the money to its investors. The first to receive payments are those who have bought notes in the "senior" tranche, after which the money is disbursed to investors in the "mezzanine" level, and so on. It may once again prove difficult for the bank to find investors for the "junior" or "unrated" tranches of the securities, but no matter: the process of securitization can be repeated as needed. A third level is thus created as mortgage-backed securities are combined into yet another pool of assets, which is once again securitized—this time as so-called Collateralized Debt Obligations. Throughout this process, mind you, the underlying mortgages remain as dodgy as ever and the possibility of default is in no way eliminated, but the logic of securitization—along with its legal architecture—does make it possible, in principle, for the risk associated with these loans to be apportioned and distributed to those who are both willing and able to shoulder it. The initial borrowers remain exposed to the elements and stand potentially to lose their houses, but thanks to the wonders of securitization, the lenders, at least, have found other individuals willing to bear their burden.

The fourth level of the tower, finally, is made up of the synthetic CDO proper—a product that, much like the standard CDO, is also sold in the form of tranches, the payments of which depend on the performance of underlying assets. Unlike the standard "cash" CDO, however (or the mortgage-backed securities that constitute it), a synthetic CDO is, well...*synthetic.* That is to say, while its portfolio may bear the risk of default associated with specific tranches of securities, it does not actually hold these tranches of securities themselves. When borrowers do default, therefore, some investors in a synthetic CDO may suffer losses as if they had invested in a cash CDO, but the underlying obligations that make up the synthetic CDO are really credit default swaps (CDSs)—that is, a type of derivative contract that was originally devised for the purpose of hedging credit risk.

The tower metaphor at this point reveals its limitations since the top layer of the synthetic CDO clearly does not "rest" on the lower levels in any conventional sense of the term. The performance of the top level may still refer to or otherwise depend on the performance of the lower levels, but the investors living in the penthouse, so to speak, do not end up suffering equally when the foundations are shaken. In fact, whereas in a cash CDO, all investors stand to benefit from a scenario in which borrowers continue to make their payments on time, regardless of what notes these investors have bought, such is not the case in a synthetic CDO. There, what one finds are really two types of investors: those who have chosen to go "long" and stand to benefit from borrowers maintaining their payment schedules and those who are instead going "short" and stand to gain from borrowers defaulting. Investors in a synthetic CDO do not all share the same interest, in other words, and they certainly do not all share the same interest as the borrowers (or as the manager of a CDO, for that matter).

What is the use of such an elaborate contraption, you ask? As Fabrice Tourre himself acknowledged in his Senate testimony, the value of such contracts "may not be obvious to the average person," but they nonetheless serve "an important need" for sophisticated investors by allowing them to "customize the exposures they wish to take" and thereby better "manage the credit and market risks of their investment holdings."[20] And in retrospect, at least, it does seem that these instruments satisfied investors' demands for AAA-rated securities. As one expert witness pointed out at Tourre's trial, there were more investment dollars in Asia than could be met by "the normal supply of treasury and AAA investment securities," and it was thus quite "sensible" for Wall Street to create new instruments. Indeed, it was something of "a natural development."[21] Others, of course, might reasonably object that this was hardly a natural development, but rather the result of prior efforts by industry lobbyists to overturn traditional regulations governing the use of so-called "difference contracts."[22] But either way, it is clear that—as the expert noted—there also developed "a second motive" for the creation of CDOs, which was to "provide an instrument for market investors who expected the U.S. housing market to collapse and who hoped to profit from it."[23]

It seems clear that in the case of John Paulson, the motives for creating a CDO were of this second type, which in turn suggests that to speak of him as an "investor" in the conventional sense may not be quite accurate. After all, what is perhaps most distinctive about synthetic CDOs is that they are derivative contracts, which is to say—as one analyst points out—that they involve "parties" and "counterparties," rather than investors per se.[24] In other words, these are deals where one party's gain is another party's loss, and while structurally speaking it may be true that a CDS or a synthetic CDO has the appearance of an insurance contract, where one party pays a regular premium, while the other commits to paying a lump sum in case of a certain "credit event," synthetic CDOs are in fact regulated differently.[25] Unlike standard insurance contracts, which allow individuals to buy protection on something they own or in which they already have a "legitimate" interest, CDSs and synthetic CDOs do not require that the parties have any ownership claim on the underlying assets. As a result, though they may be in some sense described as a form of "protection," they protect individuals only against eventualities that would otherwise not affect them. And though the original intent behind such contracts may once have been to help investors hedge volatility (rather than, say, generate an income stream), it has evidently become possible—thanks to profound technological and legal changes—for volatility itself to be treated as a source of revenue or strength, such that it would now seem—paraphrasing Max Weber—that if indeed a "spirit" of careful hedging may once have characterized the dealings of the early financiers, it has all but disappeared and has given rise instead to an iron cage of reckless speculation.[26]

BEYOND CASINO CAPITALISM: A DAY AT THE RACES?

It was John Maynard Keynes, most famously, who compared the activities of traders to games of chance and who warned against the transformation of financial markets into giant casinos.[27] The metaphor has only become more apposite, and many in recent years have decried the increasingly speculative character of contemporary finance.[28] I wonder, though, whether it might be the racetrack, rather than the casino, that provides the better metaphor—or better yet, the bettor metaphor. The racetrack, like the casino, is a place where people are making calculations and placing bets, but the bettors at a racetrack are betting on the outcome of a horse race, not that of a poker game or the spin of a wheel. In other words, they are not merely playing against each other, nor are they simply playing against the odds. They are also, and most importantly, betting on the outcome of other games being played by other players: in this case, by the horses or their jockeys.[29] Thus, when my grandfather would place his bets on a few horses every Sunday, he was not only dependent on the largesse of his lady friend Colette, who for many years subsidized his habit while my grandmother fiercely (and jealously) disapproved, he was also dependent on the competitive spirit of the jockeys and the physical prowess of the horses, without whom there would have been no race on which to bet. And, I like to think, he was also reliant on the complicity of his grandson, whom he would send on weekly errands to buy two newspapers, *Paris-Turf* and *Tiercé Magazine*, equestrian equivalents of today's credit-rating agencies, which kept him informed of the perceived strengths and popularity of all the horses that might be running on any given weekend.

In today's financial markets, likewise, when the manager of a pension fund buys or sells stocks and bonds in order to achieve a desired combination of risk and yield, he is in effect making a bet on the likelihood that their prices will rise or fall. But, if he can do this, it is only because he knows that he has at his disposal the savings of countless people—workers and pensioners alike, all of whom are planning for the future as best they can (or, as seems to be increasingly the case, planning for *their* future) and whose money he has somehow been asked to place on their behalf. Moreover, if he is able thus to "play" the stock market, it is also because he knows that there exist countless other people and institutions "out there," from individuals and corporations to (ostensibly) sovereign countries, who have also had to turn to Wall Street to finance their own needs and ambitions.

Financial markets are sites of speculation, then, where investors such as IKB, ABN AMRO, and Paulson make choices on the basis of the future they imagine. And the people whose money they are investing, likewise, are also making comparable calculations and decisions, as are the myriad borrowers on whose fortunes they are indirectly speculating. After all, not unlike the jockey who rides on the assumption that he might win the race, even the American homeowner can be seen as having made a bet: perhaps she is expecting her home will appreciate and will thus prove to be a good investment; perhaps she thinks of it as her ticket to a better school district where her children's future will be assured; or perhaps it is simply a way for her to join the American middle class or to gain citizenship in a newly constituted "ownership society."[30]

On the one hand, what all this suggests may be that today's borrowers—even the most subprime among them—are really speculators or gamblers of a sort. Yet on the other hand, they might just as easily be construed as investors in their own right—investors who in many cases may not have much to their name, but are nonetheless "sophisticated" enough to make their own choices. And indeed, that is how many of us have been told to think of ourselves in recent decades: investors one and all, individuals endowed with some amount of human capital that needs to grow. On some level, perhaps, this is nothing new. Already in the European nineteenth century, bourgeois society imagined itself as composed of individuals free and equal, all of whom had property in their person and were thus free to alienate their own labor power as they saw fit. But as we have seen, and as many others have already noted, the figure of *Homo oeconomicus* in the age of neoliberalism is not what it once was in the days of classical liberalism. Where Adam Smith imagined an individual engaged chiefly in exchange, Gary Becker and others have imagined a more competitive spirit, an "entrepreneur of the self," as Michel Foucault puts it—one who, in recent years, has been recognized as having a risk profile all his own, together with a portfolio of assets that it is both his right and responsibility to manage.[31]

There is undoubtedly a certain egalitarian promise here—an egalitarianism that binds together the denizens of the portfolio society and is naturalized by this increasingly frequent refrain, whereby the games we play are zero-sum. As one character puts it in J. C. Chandor's 2011 *Margin Call* (perhaps the best film to have come out of the financial crisis), for instance, "at the end of the day, one guy wins, the other guy loses." Except that, as his interlocutor responds (and as I hope to have shown), we "*do* know that it's a little more complicated than that, right?" On an ideological level, yes, ours may be a world where we are all investors, each of us taking and hedging risks as we see fit. But as the metaphor of the racetrack serves to remind us, the ideological cover provided by neoliberalism cannot entirely conceal the fact that investors depend on other investors in relations that are at once reciprocal and thoroughly asymmetrical. After all, if it is true that the bettors at a race track are dependent upon the jockeys, the reverse is at least as true: professional jockeys would not even exist if betting were forbidden, just as the notion of a "subprime borrower" would likely have remained a contradiction in terms if securitization and credit default swaps had not made it possible to lend money to individuals whose credit scores would otherwise have disqualified them.[32]

Financial markets are clearly structured along a class division, in other words, even if the terms of this division may sometimes be unclear: It is not a division that separates "borrowers" from "creditors" (that is admittedly how the conflict often appears, but the truth is that in this game we are all both lending and borrowing), nor is it a division that separates "sophisticated" investors from their "retail" counterparts (even if these terms are at times operative). It is, rather, a division that separates those who are free to run a race and those who are free to bet on its outcome. Or, to put it more generally yet, it would seem to be a division between those whose lives keep placing them at risk and having thus to seek protection (say, in the form of a loan or an insurance policy) and those whose position of relative security, by contrast, gives them the opportunity to take risks—say, by lending to others or betting on their probability of default.[33]

CONCLUSION: FROM VAMPIRE TO ZOMBIE?

A hundred and fifty years ago, as we have already seen, Marx described this relation—or a relation much like it—as akin to the relation between a vampire and his victim. Capital, he contended, is "dead labour which, vampire-like, lives only by sucking living labour, and

> As a capitalist, he is only capital personified. His soul is the soul of capital. But capital has one sole driving force, the drive to valorize itself, to create surplus-value, to make its constant part, the means of production, absorb the greatest possible amount of surplus labour. Capital is dead labour which, vampire-like, lives only by sucking living labour, and lives the more, the more labour it sucks. (Marx, *Capital*, vol. 1, p. 342)

lives the more, the more labour it sucks."[34] With this, Marx captured not only the violence inflicted upon the more vulnerable by the more powerful, but also—and crucially—something of the relational aspect of capital, as well as something of its compulsory nature. Indeed, much as the vampire needs to feast on the blood of a victim (after all, even a vampire has got to live), the capitalist cannot help but exploit the worker. But most importantly, perhaps—if uncertainly—what Marx's metaphor helps to convey is the fundamentally impossible and contradictory nature of the capitalist relation Marx describes: a relation the logic of which can be grasped only through a reference to the supernatural.[35]

In recent years, both in the United States and elsewhere, the language of vampirism has returned—as exemplified by Matt Taibbi's now famous description of Goldman Sachs as a "great vampire squid wrapped around the face of humanity, relentlessly jamming its blood funnel into anything that smells like money." More than the vampire or even the vampire squid, however, it is the perhaps the zombie that has most captured the imagination of the portfolio society. If only for this reason, it is the zombie that will hold our attention in these few final pages.

At first blush, the zombie and the vampire are rather similar creatures. Both clearly defy the categorical opposition of life and death, and both may certainly be said to convey the soulless and relentless violence that is at the heart of the capital relation. But while the zombie may be as dead and deadly as the vampire and is certainly just as terrifying, the terror it inspires or expresses is of another sort. As such, more to the point, it may well convey something of what is distinctly uncanny about contemporary financialized capitalism.

The vampire, we may recall, was a solitary figure living (after a fashion) in the ruins of a castle in the Carpathian Mountains.[36] And though by the nineteenth century this arguably meant he was already a relic of a bygone era, it was at least clear to everyone that his had been a life of great privilege. The zombie, by contrast, though hardly the most social of creatures, is known to dwell among other zombies—in what are recognizably the slave quarters of global capital. The zombie lacks the aristocratic lineage of the vampire, in other words, and though the traces of its origins in Haitian and African folklore have been largely erased from American popular culture and memory, there is no doubt in anyone's mind that it is among the most wretched of creatures.

And, in many ways, perhaps, that is precisely what makes the figure so unnerving, for while the brain-eating zombie may be just as menacing as the blood-sucking vampire (after all, which would you rather lose: your mind or your life?), it is also a figure of utter powerlessness: rather like the subprime, in fact, it appears to us as both victim and vector of our common affliction.[37] What is more, where the vampire seemed at least to embody an uncanny form of life—one that lived on forever, so long as it could rob other people of their own life blood, the horror of the zombie would seem to derive instead from the fact that it embodies an uncanny form of death: a death that simply refuses to die and grows the more, the more people it infects. And therein lies, finally, the true genius of zombies and financialization alike, since—as we have seen—the latter feeds not off the blood and sweat of individuals per se, but preys instead on the brains and the relations that constitute them, enlisting ever-growing populations in its expansion, implicating them and contaminating them along the way.

In light of this, one can only wonder: Is financialization—like the zombie—a menace against which society is to protect itself, or might it be the opposite, whereby both are monstrous results of a society seeking desperately to protect itself against future catastrophes? These are not questions that admit of easy answers, and I hesitate to dwell too long in this particular idiom, lest it render us even more vulnerable to the injunction to securitize—an injunction that seems almost to define the contemporary mode of prediction and protection. Perhaps it is better to give the last word to Fabrice Tourre, then, since it was he who described "all these complex, highly leveraged, exotic trades" as "monstruosities" of his own creation, and it was he who ultimately took the blame. But more importantly, it was Tourre who, in another e-mail, reflected with a mix of pride and terror on his own role in the creation of a product that—by his own account—was nothing but "a pure product of intellectual masturbation, the kind of thing you invent while telling yourself: 'what if we created a "thing" that is utterly useless, that is completely conceptual and highly theoretical, and that no one knows how to price [un "machin"...que personne ne sait pricer]?'"[38] It made him "sick to his stomach," he confided to his friend, "to see that it [was] imploding in midflight." It was "a bit like [F]rankenstein turning against his inventor."[39]

In a world that is governed by the efficient market hypothesis and where everything has a price, the creation of such a "thing" was no mere fraud: it was either a theoretical impossibility or the work of black magic. It was a true "monstruosity," in other words, one for which Tourre would eventually have to account. But if in the end Tourre's e-mails did prove incriminating, I cannot help but wonder whether they might not also contain a sliver of hope: a fleeting moment of unguarded introspection, a recognition that something is amiss. Who knows: it does seem doubtful that Tourre was all that concerned with the fate of "the poor little subprime borrowers" or of the countless European investors whose savings would soon disappear as ABACUS imploded, but surely he was right to be disturbed—worried, even. After all, if a thing cannot be priced, perhaps it is because it is not really a "thing." Perhaps it is because...because... *It's alive!*

Acknowledgments

It was Paul Samuelson, the economist, who once described Karl Marx as both "a minor post-Ricardian" and "an autodidact." I know he did not mean this as high praise, but I do like to think of myself in similar terms: as a minor post-Marxist, that is, and very much an autodidact. My education in the workings of finance, in particular, has been haphazard and mostly unguided; my earlier study of Marx, thankfully, was more supervised. But to say I have had to teach myself does not mean I have had to work alone. On the contrary, it only means I have had to rely on the patience and generosity of countless others, whose kindness I should like here to acknowledge. Nicolas Bouleau and Kate Zaloom, for instance, helped me in more ways than I care to admit. The same goes for Geoff Mann, Hadas Weiss, and Antonio Vázquez-Arroyo, who, for all their loyalty to Marx, seem to have missed his point about the "ruthless criticism of everything existing." Their criticism is of the most gentle kind.

In an airport lounge many years ago, the late Randy Martin gave me courage. Like so many others, I owe him a great deal. I also owe a great deal to his friend Bob Meister, who introduced me to a community of scholars who have enriched this project enormously. They include Edward LiPuma, Arjun Appadurai, Robert Wosnitzer, and many more. The Critical Finance Studies group in Amsterdam and Copenhagen, likewise, has provided many friends with whom to try out new ideas (or recycle old ones). At an earlier stage, Louise Amoore's conference in Durham did much the same. My thanks also to the Critical Social Theory group at McGill University and to the Social Theory Workshop at the University of Chicago. For help and comments in these and other venues, I am particularly grateful to Jacqui Ignatova, Adam Sitze, Nicolas Jabko, Joyce Goggin, Ole Bjerg, Claes Ohlsson, Natalie Roxburgh, Emily Rosamond, Benjamin Lozano, Matthew Haigh, Peter Pelzer, Emma Dowling, Joe Deville, Yves Winter, Katherine Lemons, William Clare Roberts, Gavin Walker, Hasana Sharp, Setrag Manoukian, Fabian Arzuaga, and Moishe Postone. As the book's last chapter will attest, Marieke de Goede deserves a sentence of her own. I should acknowledge also that Chapter Three first appeared as "'Moneybags Must Be So Lucky': Inside the Hidden Abode of Production," *Political Theory* 44.1 (February 2016), pp. 4–25. An earlier version of Chapter Four appeared as "The Subprime Subject of Ideology" in Kennan Ferguson and Patrice Petro (eds.), *After Capitalism: Horizons of Finance, Culture, and Citizenship* (New Brunswick, NJ: Rutgers University Press, 2016).

In the course of writing this book, I have been fortunate enough to find not one but two academic homes. At the University of Massachusetts–Amherst, I leaned on and learned from countless colleagues, many of whom ended up shaping the argument in various ways. The latter include Claire Brault, Andrés Henao Castro, Matthew Lepori, Tyler Navoichick, Mike Stein, Amel Ahmed, Barbara Cruikshank, Fred Schaffer, Nick Xenos, and Angélica Bernal. My political science colleagues at the University of Wisconsin–Milwaukee, likewise, have been unfailing in their support and have indulged me in longer conversations than mere courtesy would have required. I owe particular thanks (and apologies) to Dave Armstrong, Kathy Dolan, Kennan Ferguson, Tom Holbrook, Joel Rast, John Reuter, Paru Shah, and Natasha Borges Sugiyama. My heartfelt thanks also to Patrice Petro, Richard

Grusin, and their colleagues at the Center for International Education and the Center for Twenty-First Century Studies. I hope that others will continue to benefit from the kind of material support and intellectual community such centers are able to provide. My own community included Emily Clark, Gloria Kim, John Blum, Tracy Buss, Rachel Buff, Bernard Perley, Carolyn Eichner, Scott Graham, Joe Austin, Nigel Rothfels, Elana Levine, Stuart Moulthrop, Tasha Oren, Jason Puskar, and Mark Vareschi. *Extra muros*, my thinking for this book was shaped by conversations with Erica Bornstein, Aneesh Aneesh, Aims McGuinness, and many others. The mere fact that Annie McClanahan will likely find this book to be irksome gives me some hope there might be something here.

Closer to home, I have relied on encouragement by Mira Hayes, John Hayes, Meghan Scott, Sebastian Schmaling, Kevin Kane, Pat Buckley, and Rose Champagne. In another time and place, I relied enormously on Claudia Cumes, Chandler Klose, Michele Kunitz, Tony Tuck, Sally Staub, and Adrian Staub. And for many years now, I have turned to certain old friends for insights and sage advice. They include Daniel Kronenfeld, Robyn Marasco, Eric Snoey, Susanne Wengle, Jason Koenig, Shalini Satkunanandan, Sanjay Narayan, Jake Kosek, Oisín Curran, Dinah Rosenberg, Frédéric Keck, Marc-Antoine Blain, Matt Smith, Martin Puchner, and Amanda Claybaugh.

Finally, the *sine qua non*. The mere existence of this book is proof of what I owe to Michel Feher, who a few years ago invited me to contribute a volume to Zone's *Near Futures* series. My debt to Wendy Brown—the series' co-editor (and, in another life, my dissertation advisor)—is already a matter of public record. Such is not the case, however, of my debt to the press's anonymous reviewers. I trust that they, at least, already know how much this book owes to them. The same might be said of Meighan Gale, Ramona Naddaff, and Julie Fry, who together saw the book through its final stages. As for Bud Bynack, he not only improved my prose; he also cured me (almost) of an excessive penchant for italics. He deleted them *two hundred and thirty-one times.* And I am not even kidding.

As for my family—my parents, my brother, my wife and my children, my uncles and aunts, my cousins and my in-laws, my niece and nephew, and all those in between who have made me who I am—the debts I owe to them are almost painful to record, so keenly are they felt. Those who know me, thankfully, will already understand how much I owe to Milo, to Mattias, and above all to Anne. She is my anchor. As for my parents, JacSue and Philippe, *n'en parlons pas.* I could go on, but this is getting difficult. My father-in-law, Chuck Pycha, passed away while this page was still waiting to be finished. I still have not found the words to express my gratitude to him, or to Marguerite. And so, instead, I close with a mention of two of my uncles, Bertrand Lévy and François Ascher, to whose memory this book is dedicated. Bertrand was a banker, you see, and a man of unwavering integrity. He spoke with a certain *gravitas,* and it was he who—in my parents' kitchen—first explained to me the growing importance of credit rating agencies. François, who was about ten years his junior, was a sociologist and something of a Marxist—but of the most playful kind. In our last conversation, I remember well, he told me to write this book. He also made fun of my obsession with Marx's use of the equal sign. I miss them both immensely.

Notes

PREFACE: THE SPECTER OF WALL STREET

1. See Karl Marx and Friedrich Engels, *The Manifesto of the Communist Party*, in Karl Marx and Frederick Engels, *Collected Works* (hereafter *MECW*) (London: Lawrence and Wishart, 1976), vol. 6, p. 481. The full text of the pontiff's exhortation of November 24, 2013, *Evangelii Gaudium*, is available online at http://w2.vatican.va/content/francesco/en/apost_exhortations/documents/papa-francesco_esortazione-ap_20131124_evangelii-gaudium.html.

2. Matt Taibbi, "Inside the Great American Bubble Machine," *Rolling Stone*, July 9–23, 2009, p. 52; Warren Buffett, Letter to the Shareholders of Berkshire Hathaway Inc., 2002, p. 15. Available online at http://www.berkshirehathaway.com/letters/2002pdf.pdf.

3. Hollande's declaration was made in January 2012, while he was still running for president. Some say he has become rather more conciliatory toward finance since taking office. See Nicolas Cori, "Hollande et la finance, une volte-face en sept pas," *Libération*, July 15, 2014.

4. Pleased as I am with this formulation, I cannot claim to be entirely original. See the recent book by Joseph Vogl, *The Specter of Capital*, trans. Joachim Redner and Robert Savage (Stanford: Stanford University Press, 2014).

5. On the dangers of portraying capitalism in too frightening a fashion, see J. K. Gibson-Graham, *The End of Capitalism (As We Knew It)* (London: Blackwell, 1996).

6. There already exist countless accounts of the crisis and the years leading

up to it. I have drawn much from Robin Blackburn, "The Subprime Crisis," *New Left Review* 50 (March–April, 2008), pp. 63–106; Frédéric Lordon, *Jusqu'à quand?: Pour en finir avec les crises financières* (Paris: Liber Raisons d'agir, 2008); André Orléan, *De l'euphorie à la panique: Penser la crise financière* (Paris: Éditions de la rue d'Ulm, 2009); David Harvey, *The Enigma of Capital and the Crises of Capitalism* (Oxford: Oxford University Press, 2010); Bethany McLean and Joe Nocera, *All the Devils Are Here: The Hidden History of the Financial Crisis* (New York: Penguin, 2010); Michael Lewis, *The Big Short: Inside the Doomsday Machine* (New York: Norton, 2010); John Lanchester, *I.O.U.: Why Everyone Owes Everyone and No One Can Pay* (New York: Simon and Schuster, 2010); Leo Panitch, Greg Albo, and Vivek Chibber, eds., *The Crisis This Time: Socialist Register 2011* (London: Merlin Press, 2010); *The Financial Crisis Inquiry Report* (New York: Public Affairs, 2011); and Craig Calhoun and Georgi Derluguian, eds., *Business as Usual: The Roots of the Global Financial Meltdown* (New York: New York University Press, 2011).

7. The notion of a "portfolio society" is one I borrow from Gerald F. Davis, *Managed by the Markets: How Finance Re-Shaped America* (Oxford: Oxford University Press, 2009), p. 6. As for "financialization," a term that I will also use throughout, my debts are more diffuse. As Randy Martin points out, it is a term that tends to get "stretched and pulled in myriad directions." For Robin Blackburn, it "can most simply be defined as the growing and systemic power of finance and financial engineering." Gerald Epstein likewise defines it as "the increasing role of financial motives, financial markets, financial actors and financial institutions in the operation of the domestic and international economics." Perhaps the most widely cited definition, however, is one proposed by Greta Krippner, for whom financialization is "a pattern of accumulation in which profits accrue primarily through financial channels rather than through trade and commodity production." See Randy Martin, *Financialization of Daily Life* (Philadelphia: Temple University Press, 2002), p. 9; Robin Blackburn, "Finance and the Fourth Dimension," *New Left Review* 39 (May–June 2006), p. 39; Gerald Epstein, ed., *Financialization and the World Economy* (Northampton: Edward Elgar, 2005), p. 3; and Greta Krippner, *Capitalizing on Crisis: The*

Political Origins of the Rise of Finance (Cambridge, MA: Harvard University Press, 2011), p. 174.

8. As Vinod Kothari succinctly puts it in an otherwise lengthy tome, "'securitization' in its widest sense implies every process that converts a financial relation into a transaction." A share in a company is a prime instance of securitization, therefore, in that "ownership of a company" is a relation that is "packaged as a transaction by the creation of the ordinary share." More recently, of course, the term has also acquired a more restricted meaning, referring as it does to "a device of structured financing in which an entity seeks to pool together its interest in identifiable cash flows over time, transfer the same to investors either with or without the support of further collaterals, and thereby achieve the purpose of financing." Kothari's own focus is on this latter understanding of the term, but his initial framing is a most helpful one. See Vinod Kothari, *Securitization: The Financial Instrument of the Future* (Hoboken, NJ: John Wiley and Sons, 2006), pp. 4–9. Needless to say, not everyone shares Kothari's Pollyannaish enthusiasm for these techniques. Alain Supiot, for instance, observes that while the "commodification of human beings was long confined to workers," it has now been "extended to all types of creditor or debtor by means of innovative financial instruments. Not only can these new instruments convert an interpersonal relationship into a tradable product, but they also do away with any connection to the people engaged in the relationship. Influenced by their economic perspective on law, business lawyers have spent the past two decades actively pleading for such dissolution of people into the category of 'things.'" See Alain Supiot, "A Legal Perspective on the Economic Crisis of 2008," *International Labour Review* 149.2 (2010), p. 155. My own argument is not so dissimilar.

9. The story has been told by many others already, but the tale of the "thirty Geneva maidens" and their importance in the history of securitization is too good to pass up. It goes back to a time when savvy bankers in Geneva had the idea of purchasing annuities from the French state in the name of young Swiss girls whom they knew to be well provided for and of bundling together twenty, thirty, or forty such policies to issue securities to anyone who might want a

share of this steady income. There was always the possibility, of course, that some of these women—even of high birth—might die before their time. But the fact that the annuities had been combined meant that one girl's potential misfortune would only minimally affect the policy subscribers—so long, at least, as the French state was still able and willing to make good on its obligations. The trick worked for awhile, but then history intervened; the French Revolution took a toll on the finances of the French government, which in 1797 ended up defaulting on much of its debt. See Daniel Defert, "'Popular Life' and Insurance Technology," in Graham Burchell, Colin Gordon, and Peter Miller (eds.), *The Foucault Effect: Studies in Governmentality* (Chicago: University of Chicago Press, 1991), especially pp. 216–18. See also Charles P. Kindleberger, *A Financial History of Western Europe*, 2nd ed. (Oxford: Oxford University Press, 1993) pp. 212–13, and Dimitris P. Sotiropoulos, John Milios, and Spyros Lapatsioras, *A Political Economy of Contemporary Capitalism and its Crisis: Demystifying Finance* (London: Routledge, 2013), pp. 108–109.

10. Harry Markowitz, "Portfolio Selection," *Journal of Finance* 7.1 (March 1952), pp. 77–91. I speak of "Anglo-American capitalism" to make clear that mine is not a study of capitalism *tout court*, despite its seemingly universalizing cast. Whether "Anglo-American capitalism" is the best choice of terms by which to designate my object is another matter. I am tempted to speak even more generally of the North Atlantic zone or the Global North, but the truth is that the denizens of today's portfolio society are just as likely to reside in Dubai, Moscow, or Shanghai as in certain suburbs of Paris or Brussels.

11. The market portfolio is a portfolio composed of all risky securities. See William F. Sharpe, "Capital Asset Prices: A Theory of Market Equilibrium under Conditions of Risk," *Journal of Finance* 19.3 (September 1964), pp. 425–42. See also William F. Sharpe, "Capital Asset Prices with and without Negative Holdings," Nobel Lecture, December 7, 1990, in Karl-Göran Mäler (ed.), *Nobel Lectures, Economics 1981–1990* (Singapore: World Scientific Publishing 1992), pp. 312–32.

12. I say much too little in this book about the role of the state, whether in authorizing or in shaping the process of financialization over the last forty

years. I could perhaps produce some explanations for this neglect, having to do with my choice of *Capital* as source of inspiration; but none would really suffice. For a discussion of the political origins of financialization in the United States, see Greta Krippner, *Capitalizing on Crisis: The Political Origins of the Rise of Finance*. For a discussion of the regulatory politics leading up to the subprime crisis, specifically, see Jennifer S. Taub, *Other People's Houses: How Decades of Bailouts, Captive Regulators, and Toxic Bankers Made Home Mortgages a Thrilling Business* (New Haven: Yale University Press, 2014). For a brief description of the role of the state in the French case, see Olivier Godechot, *Les traders* (Paris: La Découverte, 2001), pp. 49–56; and for an ethnographically informed discussion of the legal infrastructure of global financial markets, see Annelise Riles, *Collateral Knowledge: Legal Reasoning in the Global Financial Markets* (Chicago: University of Chicago Press, 2011).

13. When speaking earlier of "intellectual and technological advances," I meant to evoke both the progress made in the theoretical models for the pricing of options and the myriad technologies that have helped make these models practicable. The role of the hand-held Texas Instrument calculator in popularizing the use of the Black-Scholes-Merton model is one example, but countless other developments could also be mentioned. As Donald MacKenzie points out, one development "of particular practical importance was the binomial model elaborated in Cox, Ross, and Rubinstein (1979), which especially lent itself to computerized numerical solution." See Donald MacKenzie, "Is Economics Performative?," in Donald MacKenzie, Fabian Muniesa, and Lucia Siu (eds.), *Do Economists Make Markets?: On the Performativity of Economics* (Princeton, NJ: Princeton University Press, 2007), p. 59. For a history of modern finance more generally, see Peter Bernstein, *Capital Ideas: The Improbable Origins of Modern Wall Street* (New York: Free Press, 1992), and Bernstein, *Capital Ideas Evolving* (Hoboken, NJ: John Wiley and Sons, 2007); Donald MacKenzie, *An Engine, Not a Camera: How Financial Models Shape Markets* (Cambridge, MA: MIT Press, 2006); Justin Fox, *The Myth of the Rational Market: A History of Risk, Reward, and Delusion on Wall Street* (New

York: HarperCollins, 2009); and John Cassidy, *How Markets Fail: The Logic of Economic Calamities* (New York: Farrar, Straus and Giroux, 2009).

14. See the Royal Swedish Academy of Sciences, "Press Release," October 16, 1990, available at http://www.nobelprize.org/nobel_prizes/economic-sciences/laureates/1990/press.html.

15. See MacKenzie, *An Engine, Not a Camera*, p. 92.

16. Some figures may help illustrate the trend, at least as concerns the United States. In 1950, financial sector profits accounted for about 8 percent of overall U.S. profits; by 2007, they accounted for 41 percent of corporate profits. In 1952 (the year of Markowitz's landmark publication on portfolio selection), a mere 4.2 percent of the U.S. population owned any corporate stock; by 2008, over 60 percent of U.S. adults had money in the stock market, whether directly or indirectly through mutual funds and pension funds. As for the total level of debt, which stood at roughly $10 trillion when Alan Greenspan became chairman of the Federal Reserve in 1985, it reached $43 trillion by the time he retired in 2005. The 1952 figures are from Lewis H. Kimmel, *Share Ownership in the United States* (Washington, DC: Brookings Institution, 1952), cited in Lawrence Mitchell, "Financialism: A (Very) Brief History," in Peer Zumbansen and Cynthia Williams (eds.), *The Embedded Firm* (Cambridge: Cambridge University Press, 2011), p. 47. The figures for 2008 are from Gallup's annual Economics and Personal Finance Survey, available at http://www.gallup.com/poll/182816/little-change-percentage-americans-invested-market.aspx. The figures regarding corporate profits and debt are from Michael Konczal, "Frenzied Financialization," *Washington Monthly*, November–December 2014, available at http://www.washingtonmonthly.com/magazine/novemberdecember_2014/features/frenzied_financialization052714.php, and David McNally, *Global Slump: The Economics and Politics of Crisis and Resistance* (Oakland, CA: PM Press, 2011), p. 86.

17. For a pointed critique of George W. Bush's "ownership society," see Susanne Soederberg, "Freedom, Ownership, and Social (In-)Security in the United States," *Cultural Critique* 65 (Fall 2007), pp. 92–114.

18. For a suggestive discussion of "leverage" and of debt as its underside,

see Fiona Allon, "Everyday Leverage, or Leveraging the Everyday," *Cultural Studies* 29.5–6 (2015), pp. 687–706.

19. Karl Marx, *Capital: A Critique of Political Economy*, vol. 1, trans. Ben Fowkes (New York: Penguin, 1990), p. 89.

20. *Ibid.*, p. 90; Karl Marx, *Das Kapital*, in *Marx-Engels Gesamtausgabe* II.5 (Dietz Verlag: Berlin, 1983), p. 12 (hereafter *MEGA* II.5).

21. Marx, *Capital*, vol. 1, p. 89. Robert Meister makes a similar move when he asks, as the premise for a recent seminar: "Can a project like Marx's be restated for the twenty-first century using the option, rather than the commodity, as the kernel of value?" Robert Meister, "Anthropology 268A: Rethinking Capitalism (A)" (seminar, University of California, Santa Cruz, February 2011). The short answer would have to be yes. As Merton Miller points out in his own account of the "options revolution" ushered in by the Black-Scholes pricing model, "every security can be thought of as a package of component Arrow-Debreu state-price contingent claims (options, for short), just as every physical object is a package of component atoms and molecules." Merton Miller, "A History of Finance: An Eyewitness Account," *Journal of Portfolio Management* 13.2 (Summer 1999), p. 101. Marx would have enjoyed the metaphor, even if he understood that "in the analysis of economic forms neither microscopes nor chemical reagents are of assistance." See Marx, *Capital*, vol. 1, p. 90. In a different but related vein, see the work of Joseph Dumit, "Prescription Maximization and the Accumulation of Surplus Health in the Pharmaceutical Industry: The_BioMarx_Experiment," in Kaushik Sunder Rajan (ed.), *Lively Capital: Biotechnologies, Ethics, and Governance in Global Markets* (Durham, NC: Duke University Press, 2012), pp. 45–92.

CHAPTER ONE: CAPITALISM

1. For the detail of some of Tourre's e-mails, see Steve Eder and Karey Wutkowski, "Goldman's 'Fabulous' Fab's Conflicted Love Letters," Reuters, April 26, 2010, available at http://www.reuters.com/article/2010/04/26/us-goldman-emails-idUSTRE63O26E20100426, and "Les mails étonnants de Fabrice Tourre," *L'Express*, L'Expansion.com, April 26, 2010, available at http://

lexpansion.lexpress.fr/entreprises/les-mails-etonnants-de-fabrice-tourre_
1449864.html. The "dinosaur" reference is from Fabrice Tourre's e-mail to
Fatiha Boukhtouche, January 31, 2007.

2. In his tell-all description of life at Goldman Sachs, Greg Smith describes
Tourre as a "classic quant," "slightly goofy" and "socially awkward," who had
clearly "not been hired on the strength of his charisma." Greg Smith, *Why I Left
Goldman Sachs: A Story of Wall Street* (New York: Grand Central Publishing,
2012), chapter 9. Who knows: perhaps he was hired because he was French;
according to one analyst at least, "about a third of 'quants' working in the world"
are graduates "from French business schools," and "top institutions without a
French person at the helm or in the ranks of the research and studies department are rare." See David Sitbon, "French Excellence in Quantitative Finance
Should Benefit French Banks," Keyrus Capital Markets, n.d., p. 2, available as a
PDF via a Google search. This particular statement seems implausible, if only
because it elides the importance of French engineering schools and other
Grandes Écoles, but the basic point is well taken: a disproportionate number of
quantitative analysts hail from France, for reasons that would deserve a study of
their own. For now, suffice it to say that the influence of Nicole El Karoui's
teaching is well established. (See, for instance, Carrick Mollenkamp and
Charles Fleming, "Why Students of Prof. El Karoui Are In Demand," *Wall Street
Journal*, March 9, 2006, and Annie Kahn, "Nicole El Karoui, la boss des
maths," *Le Monde*, May 15, 2006. Further insights can be gleaned from the
work of Nicolas Bouleau (himself a former professor of mathematical finance at
the École des Ponts) and from Françoise Balibar's reflections on the teaching of
science in French institutions of higher learning, "De l'homme sans qualités au
trader," available online at http://philolarge.hypotheses.org/432.

3. I have in mind both the repeal of the Glass-Steagall Act in 1999 (or more
precisely, the passage of the Gramm-Leach-Bliley Act) and the passage of the
Commodity Futures Modernization Act in 2000. On the latter, see Lynn Stout,
"Derivatives and the Legal Origins of the 2008 Crisis," *Harvard Business Law
Review* 1 (2011), pp. 1–38. On the repeal of Glass-Steagall and related matters,
see, for instance, the work of Steven A. Sibo, "Credit Default Swaps: How

Should They Be Regulated?" (July 3, 2012). Available at the Social Science Research Network, http://ssrn.com/abstract=2099886.

4. The figures for the home ownership rate are those of the U.S. Census Bureau. In 2001, according to Jennifer Taub, "$190 billion in subprime loans were originated and $87 billion in bonds for pools of subprime loans were issued. Five years later, there was $600 billion in subprime origination and $448.6 billion in issuance." Jennifer S. Taub, "The Sophisticated Investor and the Global Crisis," in James P. Hawley, Shyam J. Kamath, and Andrew T. Williams (eds.), *Corporate Governance Failures: The Role of Institutional Investors in the Global Financial Crisis* (Philadelphia: University of Pennsylvania Press, 2011), p. 208.

5. David Harvey, *The Enigma of Capital and the Crises of Capitalism* (Oxford: Oxford University Press, 2010), p. 1.

6. See Neal Deckant, "Criticisms of Collateralized Debt Obligations in the Wake of the Goldman Sachs Scandal," *Review of Banking and Financial Law* 30.1 (2010–2011), p. 422.

7. Gillian Tett, "The Unease Bubbling in Today's Brave New Financial World," *Financial Times*, January 19, 2007, available at http://www.ft.com/cms/s/0/92f7ee6a-a765-11db-83e4-0000779e2340.html.

8. *Ibid.*

9. Fabrice Tourre to Marine Serres, e-mail dated January 23, 2007.

10. Fabrice Tourre to Marine Serres, e-mail dated March 7, 2007.

11. *Ibid.*

12. See Harvey, *The Enigma of Capital*, p. 6.

13. Clinton's eloquent phrase is reported in Bob Woodward, *The Agenda* (New York: Simon and Schuster, 1994), p. 73.

14. For a discussion of the "crisis narrative" in general and its deployment in the context of the subprime crisis, specifically, see Janet Roitman, *Anti-Crisis* (Durham, NC: Duke University Press, 2014), pp. 41–70. Needless to say, mine is hardly a comprehensive survey of the narratives on offer. My point is simply to highlight some of the ways in which the recent crisis has foregrounded the apparent "monstrosity" of contemporary capitalism.

15. For some, the quants' tragic flaw was to have believed that they could predict the future on the basis of the past. Thus, according to Nassim Nicholas Taleb, for instance, it was foolish indeed to think that no "black swans" would ever be encountered, simply because none had been seen before. For others, the quants' crucial mistake was to have assumed that individual stock prices (and, more to the point, individual mortgages) move randomly and independently from each other, when in fact, they manifestly do not. For others yet, it was an epistemological confusion between theories and models that was to blame, along with an excessive mathematization of finance and all the obfuscation it enabled. But in each of these cases, the verdict was much the same: the quants had either convinced themselves or convinced everyone else that they had found the philosopher's stone, and the rest of us ended up either "fooled by randomness" or fooled by those who had claimed to conquer it. See, for instance, Benoît Mandelbrot and Richard L. Hudson, *The (Mis)Behavior of Markets: A Fractal View of Financial Turbulence* (New York: Basic Books, 2004); Nassim Nicholas Taleb, *Fooled by Randomness: The Hidden Role of Chance in Life and in the Markets* (New York: Random House, 2004), and Taleb, *The Black Swan: The Impact of the Highly Improbable* (New York: Random House, 2007); Riccardo Rebonato, *Plight of the Fortune Tellers: Why We Need to Manage Financial Risk Differently* (Princeton, NJ: Princeton University Press, 2007); Henri Bourguinat and Éric Briys, *L'arrogance de la finance: Comment la théorie financière a produit le krach* (Paris: La Découverte, 2009); Emanuel Derman, *Models. Behaving. Badly.: Why Confusing Illusion with Reality Can Lead to Disaster, on Wall Street and in Life* (New York: Free Press, 2011); Nicolas Bouleau, "Can There Be Excessive Mathematization of the World?," *Progress in Probability* 67 (2013), pp. 453–69. Many of these arguments, it should be noted, were made well before the crisis happened. As for Gillian Tett, her own reconstruction of the crisis and its origins suggests it was the inventiveness of a few people in J. P. Morgan's credit derivatives department that was to blame — if not for the crash itself, then for the combined use of securitization and credit default swaps that would lead both to the expansion of the derivatives market in the late 1990s and to its eventual collapse ten years later. For many years prior,

admittedly, investment banks in New York, London, and elsewhere had experimented with so-called "credit derivatives" to separate out the credit risk associated with making loans (that is, the risk that borrowers might default) and turn it into a product in its own right that could be sold on financial markets. But it was not until the late 1990s that a handful of ambitious (if raucous) young men and women at J. P. Morgan had the idea of bundling together nearly ten billion dollars' worth of loans, selling claims to most of them as highly rated tranches, and buying insurance on the remaining assets in the form of credit default swaps. This allowed credit risk to become so diffuse as to become almost invisible (at least to investors and regulators) and allowed J. P. Morgan to exceed the limits on how much money it could invest. The problems came a few years later, when countless other banks engaged in similar practices, only this time with loans of much lesser quality. See Gillian Tett, *Fool's Gold: The Inside Story of J. P. Morgan and How Wall St. Greed Corrupted Its Bold Dream and Created a Financial Catastrophe* (New York: Free Press, 2009).

16. See, for instance, David C. Korten, *Agenda for a New Economy: From Phantom Wealth to Real Wealth* (San Francisco: Berrett-Koehler, 2009).

17. As we will see, Fabrice Tourre seemed happy to invoke the figure of Frankenstein to describe his own role as a quant (even if, unlike Mary Shelley, he used the name Frankenstein to designate the creature, rather than the creator). But this is perhaps not so surprising: after all, comparing himself to the archetypal mad scientist served both to dignify his work in quantitative finance (by implying that is in fact a form of "science") while paradoxically shifting the blame onto the "creature," since by all accounts, the latter ended up taking on "a life of its own." But whatever its meaning, one thing is sure: the Frankenstein trope is a powerful one and long predates the 2008 crisis. Already in 2000, the journalist Roger Lowenstein used it to good effect in recounting the rise and fall of Long-Term Capital Management, the ill-fated hedge fund to which Robert Merton and Myron Scholes had both lent their expertise and authority. As Lowenstein puts it, "the professors … sent their mathematical Frankenstein gamely into the world as if it could tame the element of chance in life itself. No self-doubt tempered them; no sense of

perspective checked them as they wagered such staggering sums." Roger Low-enstein, *When Genius Failed: The Rise and Fall of Long-Term Capital Management* (New York: Random House, 2000), p. 235. As for the zombie metaphor, while it is of more recent coinage than its Frankenstein equivalent, it is no less popular. See, for instance, Paul Krugman, "Wall Street Voodoo," *New York Times*, January 19, 2009, and Yalman Onaran, *Zombie Banks: How Broken Banks and Debtor Nations are Crippling the Global Economy* (Hoboken, NJ: Wiley and Sons, 2012). More critical reflections on the history and use of the concept may be found in Taylor C. Nelms, "The Zombie Bank and the Magic of Finance," *Journal of Cultural Economy* 5.2 (2012), pp. 231–46.

18. See David McNally, *Global Slump: The Economics and Politics of Crisis and Resistance* (Oakland, CA: PM Press, 2011), p. 2.

19. Robert Brenner, "Prólogo a la edición española: Los orígenes de la crisis actual. Lo que es bueno para Goldman Sachs es bueno para Estados Unidos," *La economía de la turbulencia global*, trans. Juan Mari Madariaga (Madrid: Akal, 2009), p. 24. An English version of this essay, "What is Good for Goldman Sachs Is Good for America: The Origins of the Current Crisis," was presented at the Center for Social Theory and Comparative History, University of California, Los Angeles, April 18, 2009.

20. David Harvey, "The Enigma of Capital and the Crisis This Time," paper prepared for the American Sociological Association Meetings in Atlanta, August 16, 2010, available at http://davidharvey.org/2010/08/the-enigma-of-capital-and-the-crisis-this-time.

21. See Gérard Duménil and Dominique Lévy, *The Crisis of Neoliberalism* (Cambridge, MA: Harvard University Press, 2013). For an account of how a "finance-led regime of accumulation" seems to have replaced the "Fordist" regime of accumulation of the postwar years, see Robert Boyer, *Les financiers détruiront-ils le capitalisme?* (Paris: Economica, 2011).

22. Karl Marx, *Capital: A Critique of Political Economy*, vol. 1, trans. Ben Fowkes (New York: Penguin, 1990), pp. 342 and 926. See David McNally, *Monsters of the Market: Zombies, Vampires and Global Capitalism* (Leiden: Brill, 2011), and Chris Harman, *Zombie Capitalism* (Chicago: Haymarket, 2010).

23. See Marx, *Capital*, vol. 1, p. 92. There is nothing new about turning to Marx to understand finance, but not all of us do it in quite the same way. Like Miranda Joseph, "I join Dick Bryan, Randy Martin, and Mike Rafferty...in understanding financialization as 'a development within rather than a distortion of capitalist production,' which nonetheless has specific and 'extensive' 'ramifications' worthy of investigation and explication." See Miranda Joseph, *Debt to Society: Accounting for Life Under Capitalism* (Minneapolis: University of Minnesota Press, 2014), p. 2, and Dick Bryan, Randy Martin, and Mike Rafferty, "Financialization and Marx: Giving Labor and Capital a Financial Makeover," *Review of Radical Political Economics* 41.4 (December, 2009) pp. 458–72. I have also learned much from the following works, each of which beautifully combines a reading of Marx with a reading of finance: Edward LiPuma and Benjamin Lee, *Financial Derivatives and the Globalization of Risk* (Durham, NC: Duke University Press, 2004); Dick Bryan and Michael Rafferty, *Capitalism with Derivatives: A Political Economy of Financial Derivatives, Capital and Class* (New York: Palgrave Macmillan, 2006); Jonathan Nitzan and Shimshon Bichler, *Capital as Power: A Study of Order and Creorder* (New York: Routledge, 2009); Dimitris P. Sotiropoulos, John Milios, and Spyros Lapatsioras, *A Political Economy of Contemporary Capitalism and its Crisis: Demystifying Finance* (London: Routledge, 2013); Max Haiven, *Cultures of Financialization: Fictitious Capital in Popular Culture and Everyday Life* (London: Palgrave Macmillan, 2014); Susanne Soederberg, *Debtfare States and the Poverty Industry: Money, Discipline and the Surplus Population* (London: Routledge, 2014); Cédric Durand, *Le capital fictif: Comment la finance s'approprie notre avenir* (Paris: Les Prairies ordinaires, 2014); the chapters by Randy Martin and Robert Meister in the collaborative effort of Arjun Appadurai, Elie Ayache, Emanuel Derman, Benjamin Lee, Edward LiPuma, Randy Martin, Robert Meister, and Robert Wosnitzer, *Derivatives and the Wealth of Societies* (Chicago: University of Chicago Press, forthcoming).

24. The idea that human beings are "forward-looking," at the very least, is a basic assumption of modern economics. Gary S. Becker, for one, is happy to assume that "individuals maximize welfare *as they conceive it*.... Their behavior

is forward-looking. In particular, they try as best they can to anticipate the uncertain consequences of their actions." Gary S. Becker, "The Economic Way of Looking at Life," Nobel Lecture, December 9, 1992, in Torsten Persson (ed.), *Nobel Lectures, Economics 1991–1995* (Singapore: World Scientific Publishing, 1997), p. 38. But the fact that people have always looked "forward" does not mean they have always done it in the same way. Take Hamlet, for instance. In Shakespeare's day, the young prince lived in a rotten country where even a king could be killed at any moment (and in the strangest of fashions, to boot). No wonder he became a bit of a worrywart and a recluse who variously complained about the "slings and arrows of outrageous Fortune" and worried aloud about "what dreams may come" if, for some reason, he should decide to put an end to it all. His conscience was enough to make him a coward who in the end did not amount to much. (Not only did he die, but he brought everyone else down with him.) But by the time Hamlet returned to us as *The Lion King* in the mid-1990s (that is, before Clinton's Personal Responsibility and Work Opportunity Act of 1996, also known as the "end of welfare as we [had] come to know it"), he had adopted a different outlook. "Hakuna matata," he chanted: "it means 'no worries.'" And though he was still a born aristocrat and not inclined to industry, Simba did grow up in a different climate: he knew he could rely on his friends Zazu and Rafiki to help him enjoy the good life, and when push came to shove, he was also able to count on Timon, Pumbaa, and others to fend off the hyenas. The results were spectacular: not only did he get the girl (who now went by the name of Nala), but together they had a child, and the circle of life was allowed to continue. Those were the days of the welfare state. Today, things would undoubtedly look different: Simba and Nala would still be elated at the birth of an heir, but in the midst of their euphoria they would likely make sure to set aside some money for the cub's college fund and maybe sign up for life insurance, just in case.

25. Marx, *Capital*, vol. 1, p. 284. For a more recent use of the bee and its pollinating virtues as metaphor for cognitive capitalism, see Yann Moulier Boutang, *L'abeille et l'économiste* (Paris: Carnet Nord, 2010), pp. 118–29.

26. The example I have in mind is the Canary Wharf business district in

London, the financing of which is described in detail in Vinod Kothari, *Securitization: The Financial Instrument of the Future* (Hoboken, NJ: John Wiley and Sons, 2006), pp. 381–83.

27. This particular illustration works well, given Marx's evocation of the architect and the bees, but countless other examples could be adduced. Thus, Andrew Leyshon and Nigel Thrift observed in 2007 that "in the United States and now in the UK, universities have been issuing bonds based on student income streams of various kinds (for example, rental income from halls of residence) or on a share of the putative intellectual property from research." Andrew Leyshon and Nigel Thrift, "The Capitalization of Almost Everything: The Future of Finance and Capitalism," *Theory, Culture and Society* 24.7–8 (2007), p. 103. On the adoption of such practices by the University of California, specifically, see Bob Meister, "Debt and Taxes: Can the Financial Industry Save Public Universities?," *Representations* 116.1 (Fall 2011), pp. 128–55. On the political nature of such processes, see Susanne Soederberg, "Student Loans, Debtfare and the Commodification of Debt: The Politics and the Displacement of Risk," *Critical Sociology* 40.5 (September 2014), pp. 689–709.

28. On the relation between financial securitization, surveillance, and militarization, see Randy Martin, *An Empire of Indifference: American War and the Financial Logic of Risk Management* (Durham, NC: Duke University Press, 2007), pp. 17–63. On related questions regarding the links between neoliberalism and the logic of preemption, see Melinda Cooper and Martijn Konings, "Contingency and Foundation: Rethinking Money, Debt, and Finance after the Crisis," *South Atlantic Quarterly* 114.2 (April 2015), p. 247.

29. The distinctions between freeman and slave, patrician and plebeian, and so on, are from the *Manifesto*; the distinction between retail and sophisticated investors (to which I will return) is from the vernacular of contemporary finance. Suffice it to say for now that a sophisticated investor is one who is deemed knowledgeable enough—usually on the basis of her wealth—to decide for herself on the judiciousness of an investment opportunity.

30. Don't get me wrong: Thomas Piketty's *Le capital au XXIe siècle* (Paris: Seuil, 2013), available in English as Thomas Piketty, *Capital in the Twenty-*

First Century, trans. Arthur Goldhammer (Cambridge, MA: Belknap Press of Harvard University Press, 2014), is both masterful and fully deserving of its title. But it is probably true, as Geoff Mann suggests, that the more accurate comparison is not to Marx's *Capital*, but to John Maynard Keynes's *General Theory of Employment, Interest and Money* (New York: Harcourt, 1936). See Geoff Mann, "A General Theory for Our Times: On Piketty," *Historical Materialism* 23.1 (2015), pp. 106–40.

31. See Brad A. Seibel et al., "Vampire Blood: Respiratory Physiology of the Vampire Squid (Cephalopoda: Vampyromorpha) in Relation to the Oxygen Minimum Layer," *Experimental Biology Online* 4.1 (December 1999), pp. 1–10.

32. I borrow the phrase "zombie capitalism" from Harman, *Zombie Capitalism*.

33. Marx, *Capital*, vol. 1, p. 126.

34. Perhaps Marx was onto something. Louis Althusser, the most French of readers, did find the opening chapters of *Capital* unnecessarily Hegelian and advised readers of *Capital* to skip them altogether and begin with the second section, "The Transformation of Money into Capital." See Louis Althusser, "Avertissement au lecteur du Livre I du *Capital*," in Karl Marx, *Le capital, livre I* (Paris: Garnier-Flammarion, 1969).

35. Marx, *Capital*, vol. 1, p. 165.

36. *Ibid.*, p. 270. Ben Fowkes, on whose judicious translation of *Capital* I have otherwise relied throughout, soberly translates the German *Geldbesitzer* as "money-owner." For this particular word, I have opted for the more whimsical translation by Marx's son-in-law, Edward Aveling, to which Engels lent his own stamp of approval. See *MECW*, vol. 35 (London: Lawrence and Wishart, 1996), p. 176.

37. Marx, *Capital*, vol. 1, p. 165.

CHAPTER TWO: A MONSTROUS COLLECTION OF SECURITIES

1. Images of some of these bonds are available on the museum's website at http://www.moaf.org/publications-collections/museum-collection/stocks-bonds/index.

2. Karl Marx, *Capital: A Critique of Political Economy*, vol. 1, trans. Ben Fowkes (New York: Penguin, 1990), p. 163.

3. As people often do when entering into the bonds of holy matrimony, the bank formerly known as J. P. Morgan changed its name on the occasion of its merger with the Chase Manhattan Corporation in 2000. It is now JPMorgan Chase & Co.

4. I have never worked in an investment bank or in the New York Stock Exchange, but my imagination has been nourished by the painstaking ethnographic work of others, including Donald MacKenzie, *Material Markets: How Economic Agents Are Constructed* (Oxford: Oxford University Press, 2008); Caitlin Zaloom, *Out of the Pits: Traders and Technology from Chicago to London* (Chicago: University of Chicago Press, 2006); Robert Wosnitzer, "Desk, Firm, God, Country: Proprietary Trading and the Speculative Ethos of Financialism," Ph.D. diss., New York University Department of Media, Culture, and Communication, 2014; Vincent Antonin Lépinay, *Codes of Finance: Engineering Derivatives in a Global Bank* (Princeton, NJ: Princeton University Press, 2011); David Stark, *The Sense of Dissonance: Accounts of Worth in Economic Life* (Princeton, NJ: Princeton University Press, 2009); Olivier Godechot, *Les traders* (Paris: La Découverte, 2001), and Godechot, *Working Rich* (Paris: La Découverte, 2007); Karen Ho, *Liquidated: An Ethnography of Wall Street* (Durham, NC: Duke University Press, 2009); Hirokazu Miyazaki, *Arbitraging Japan: Dreams of Capitalism at the End of Finance* (Berkeley: University of California Press, 2013).

5. Marx, *Capital*, vol. 1, p. 125.

6. *Ibid.* Karl Marx, *Das Kapital*, in Marx-Engels, *MEGA* II.5, p. 17. When Marx undertook his landmark critique of political economy a hundred and fifty years ago, he worked with and against the categories of the age. It is not surprising, therefore, that there should be an echo of Adam Smith's *Wealth of Nations* in the opening lines of *Capital*. Like Smith, it seems, Marx proceeds from the assumption that the wealth of nations is measured by the amount of goods in circulation (rather than, say, by the amount of gold in the king's coffers) and like Smith, Marx presents his own analysis as "an inquiry into the nature and causes" of this wealth. See Adam Smith, *An Inquiry into the Nature*

and *Causes of the Wealth of Nations* (1776; Chicago: University of Chicago Press, 1976).

7. Marx, *Capital*, vol. 1, p. 129. See, among others, Robert Paul Wolff, *Understanding Marx: A Reconstruction and Critique of Capital* (Princeton, NJ: Princeton University Press, 1984).

8. Rare is the description of contemporary financial markets that does not comment on their gigantism. As Edward LiPuma and Benjamin Lee put it simply, "the numbers are truly staggering." Edward LiPuma and Benjamin Lee, "Financial Derivatives and the Rise of Circulation," *Economy and Society* 34.3 (August 2005), p. 406. For a discussion of the changing scale of financial markets, see Saskia Sassen, "Global Finance and Its Institutional Spaces," in Karin Knorr Cetina and Alex Preda (eds.), *The Oxford Handbook of the Sociology of Finance* (Oxford: Oxford University Press, 2012), especially pp. 20–22.

9. Marx, *Capital*, vol. 1, p. 163.

10. *Ibid.*, p. 125.

11. For a helpful reminder of the basic social functions of financial markets, see Pierre-Noël Giraud, *Le commerce des promesses* (Paris: Seuil, 2009).

12. Textbook explanations of wheat futures are easy to find, but the most precise (if somewhat argumentative) description I have encountered is that provided by Aaron Brown in his *Red-Blooded Risk: The Secret History of Wall Street* (Hoboken, NJ: John Wiley and Sons, 2012), pp. 180–83.

13. See Immanuel Wallerstein, *The Modern World System II: Mercantilism and the Consolidation of the European World-Economy, 1600–1750* (1980; Berkeley: University of California Press, 2011), chapter 2.

14. I should point out that what I am calling here "hedging value" could just as well be called "speculative value," even if the term would inevitably carry a different moral valence. As Martijn Konings points out, "in derivatives markets (typically depicted as the quintessential expression of casino capitalism), any hard-and-fast distinction between hedging and speculative financing breaks down. Risk avoidance and security become themselves speculative propositions, requiring the continuous differentiation of financial positions. Derivatives trading can be understood as responding to the absence of fundamental

values (by making risk itself a tradable commodity) and so can be seen as constituting a (paradoxical) regime of measure." Martijn Konings, "State of Speculation: Contingency, Measure, and the Politics of Plastic Value," *South Atlantic Quarterly* 114.2 (April 2015), p. 274.

15. Marx, *Capital*, vol. 1, p. 127; *MEGA* II.5, p. 19.

16. The reader will forgive me, I hope, if at times I speak of "efficiency" at some level of generality. For a careful study of the concept and its pitfalls, see Nicolas Bouleau, "Dommages et intérêt de la spéculation: Inefficience de la finance," Centre International de Recherche sur l'Environnement et le Développement, May 2013, available at https://halshs.archives-ouvertes.fr/halshs-00823520. And, by the same author, "L'efficience: Une imposture scientifique réussie? Finance et environnement," February 2013, available at http://www.univ-paris13.fr/cepn/IMG/pdf/texte_seminaire_240114.pdf.

17. For a related analysis, see LiPuma and Lee, "Financial Derivatives and the Rise of Circulation."

18. Along these lines, more or less, John Burr Williams in the late 1930s argued that the valuation of a security required both a long-run projection of its dividend payments and a judgment about that projection's accuracy. Williams recognized that not all companies are equally likely to survive, in other words, and he thought it wise to consider this uncertainty in the assessment of their stock's intrinsic worth. See John Burr Williams, *Theory of Investment Value* (Cambridge, MA: Harvard University Press, 1938), cited in Peter Bernstein, *Capital Ideas: The Improbable Origins of Modern Wall Street* (New York: Free Press, 1992), p. 31.

19. Bernstein, *Capital Ideas*, p. 47.

20. *Ibid.*, p. 81.

21. *Ibid.*, pp. 80–81.

22. Marx, *Capital*, vol. 1, p. 132; *MEGA* II.5, p. 22.

23. This calls to mind a phrase by Dick Bryan, Michael Rafferty, and Chris Jefferis: "Critically for our analysis, these calculative techniques of capital [the Black-Scholes model of options pricing and techniques of the capital asset pricing (CAPM) and value at risk (VaR)] perform the process by which discrete

investments are made mutually commensurable, and hence 'capital' itself is made homogeneous (capital in general) via the concept of return relative to calculative risk." Dick Bryan, Michael Rafferty, and Chris Jefferis, "Risk and Value: Finance, Labor, and Production," *South Atlantic Quarterly* 114.2 (April 2015), p. 315.

24. Indeed in 1973, options could still be described as "specialized and relatively unimportant financial securities." See Robert Merton, "Theory of Rational Option Pricing," *Bell Journal of Economics and Management Science* 4.1 (Spring 1973), p. 14. See also Ole Bjerg, *Making Money: The Philosophy of Crisis Capitalism* (London: Verso, 2014), p. 198.

25. See Nicolas Bouleau, *Martingales et marchés financiers* (Paris: Odile Jacob, 1998), available in English as Nicolas Bouleau, *Financial Markets and Martingales: Observations on Science and Speculation*, trans. Alan Thomas (London: Springer, 2004).

26. The Black-Scholes-Merton model—and with it, almost all of modern financial theory—starts from the assumption that the fluctuations of stock are (or are akin to) a stochastic process. The botanist Robert Brown observed the movement of particles of pollen in water and noted that the movement is random. In 1900, this same notion was developed in the context of stocks by the French mathematician Louis Bachelier, who contended in his doctoral dissertation that stock prices go up and down in a random fashion. One cannot know from one moment to the next whether the price of a stock (or an index) will go up or down, but this in itself is a form of knowledge, which gives rise to a new kind of thinking. It is no longer necessary to know anything about the "fundamentals" of a company, provided one knows what the price was a moment ago: a stock's price at $t1$, more likely than not, will be roughly what it was at $t0$. For a powerful critique of this paradigm, see the work of Benoît Mandelbrot and Nassim Nicholas Taleb, among others: Benoît Mandelbrot and Richard L. Hudson, *The (Mis)Behavior of Markets: A Fractal View of Financial Turbulence* (New York: Basic Books, 2004); Nassim Nicholas Taleb, *The Black Swan: The Impact of the Highly Improbable* (New York: Random House, 2007). See also Louis Bachelier, "Théorie de la spéculation,"

Annales de l'École Normale Supérieure, 3rd series, no. 17 (Paris: Gauthier-Villars, 1900).

27. Bill Maurer, "Repressed Futures: Financial Derivatives' Theological Unconscious," *Economy and Society* 31.1 (February 2002), p. 22.

28. See Duncan Wigan, "Financialization and Derivatives: Constructing an Artifice of Indifference," *Competition and Change* 13.2 (June 2009), p. 162.

29. Fischer Black and Myron Scholes, "The Pricing of Options and Corporate Liabilities," *Journal of Political Economy* 81.3 (May–June 1973), p. 641.

30. Bjerg, *Making Money*, pp. 198–99.

31. One can only presume that Black and Scholes had at least an inkling of how influential their model might become. As Merton Miller points out, the authors made sure their title referred not only to the "pricing of options" but to that of "corporate liabilities," so that the journal's editors would recognize their contribution not merely as a "technical *tour de force* in mathematical statistics," but as "an advance with wide application for the study of market prices." See Merton Miller, "A History of Finance: An Eyewitness Account," *The Journal of Portfolio Management* 13.2 (Summer 1999), p. 101. This calls to mind the final paragraphs of James D. Watson and Francis H. C. Crick's one-page description of their own model—for the structure of DNA, this time—which reads: "It has not escaped our notice that the specific pairing we have postulated immediately suggests a possible copying mechanism for the genetic material." "Molecular Structure of Nucleic Acids: A Structure for Deoxyribose Nucleic Acid," *Nature*, April 25, 1953, p. 737.

32. I borrow the notion of a "universal financial device" from Bernstein, who borrows it from Aristotle, who in turn borrows it from Thales. See Bernstein, *Capital Ideas*, p. 203.

33. There is much more to be said, of course, about the various mystifications and absurdities that accompany securitization, including the fact that these securities are rated by agencies that have every reason to give them positive ratings. See, among others, Neal Deckant, "Criticisms of Collateralized Debt Obligations in the Wake of the Goldman Sachs Scandal," *Review of Banking and Financial Law* 30.1 (2010–2011), p. 412.

34. Marx, *Capital*, vol. 1, p. 139.

35. Many others have already written in different ways about the fetishism that is at work in financial markets. See, for instance, Bill Maurer, "Repressed Futures," p. 22; Susanne Soederberg, "Cannibalistic Capitalism: The Paradoxes of Neoliberal Pension Securitization," in Leo Panitch, Greg Albo, and Vivek Chibber (eds.), *The Crisis This Time: Socialist Register 2011* (New York: Monthly Review Press, 2010), pp. 224–41; Benjamin Lozano, *Of Synthetic Finance: Three Essays of Speculative Materialism* (London: Routledge, 2015). Ultimately, though, it was Marx himself who first recognized the fetishism that attaches to securities. As Dimitris P. Sotiropoulos, John Milios, and Spyros Lapatsioras point out, Marx "introduces the concept of fictitious capital, and speaks of fetishism, when he gives an account of the social nature of financial markets. He wants to underline the fact that capital assets are the *reified* forms of the appearance of the social relation of capital, and so their valuation is associated with a particular organic representation of capitalist relations." See Dimitris P. Sotiropoulos, John Milios, and Spyros Lapatsioras, *A Political Economy of Contemporary Capitalism and its Crisis: Demystifying Finance* (London: Routledge, 2013), p. 151.

36. Marx, *Capital*, vol. 1, p. 169.

37. Marx was not alone in poking fun at his contemporaries for relying on Robinsonades. Friedrich Engels criticized Eugen von Dühring for the same penchant, even though—as Yves Winter demonstrates—a similar critique could be made of Engels's own analysis of Dühring. See Yves Winter, "Debating Violence on the Desert Island: Engels, Dühring and Robinson Crusoe," *Contemporary Political Theory* 13.4 (November 2014), pp. 318–38.

38. Daniel Defoe, *Robinson Crusoe* (1719; New York: Aladdin, 2001), p. 285.

39. See Pensée 233 in Blaise Pascal, *Pensées* (1670; Paris: Léon Brunschvicg, 1897), pp. 55–59.

40. Defoe, *Robinson Crusoe*, p. 93.

41. *Ibid.*

42. *Ibid.*

43. For helpful discussions of the development and influence of the "value at risk" model, see Riccardo Rebonato, *The Plight of the Fortune Tellers: Why We*

Need to Manage Financial Risk Differently (Princeton, NJ: Princeton University Press, 2007), pp. 117–38; Michael Power, *Organized Uncertainty: Designing a World of Risk Management* (Oxford: Oxford University Press, 2007), pp. 71–75; Brown, *Red-Blooded Risk*, pp. 213–54.

44. The notion of a "risk society" is one I borrow from Ulrich Beck: *Risikogesellschaft: Auf dem Weg in eine andere Moderne* (Frankfurt am Main: Suhrkamp, 1986), available in English as Ulrich Beck, *Risk Society: Towards a New Modernity*, trans. Mark Ritter (London: Sage, 1992).

45. Marx, *Capital*, vol. 1, p. 170.

46. *Ibid.*

47. *Ibid.*

48. Georges Duby, *The Three Orders: Feudal Society Imagined*, trans. Arthur Goldhammer (Chicago: University of Chicago Press, 1980), p. 158.

49. Georges Duby, *Le chevalier, la femme et le prêtre* (1981; Paris: Pluriel, 2012), p. 189.

50 Duby, *The Three Orders*, p. 40.

51. *Ibid.*, p. 106.

52. Marx, *Capital*, vol. 1, p. 171.

53. *Ibid.*

54. *Ibid.*, p. 172.

55. *Ibid.*, pp. 169 and 173.

56. I am thinking for instance of the β of the stock (a measure of its volatility) or the so-called "Greeks" by which analysts characterize financial derivatives.

57. Marx, *Capital*, vol. 1, p. 169.

58. *Ibid.*

59. See Hirokazu Miyazaki, "Between Arbitrage and Speculation: An Economy of Belief and Doubt," *Economy and Society* 36.3 (2007), pp. 396–415.

CHAPTER THREE: FINDING SAFETY IN NUMBERS

1. Karl Marx, *Capital: A Critique of Political Economy*, vol. 1, trans. Ben Fowkes (New York: Penguin, 1990), p. 270.

2. Marx did not always have the best sense of timing: no sooner did he publish *Capital* than the marginalist revolution began, rejecting the very distinction between use value and exchange value on which classical political economy—and hence, Marx's critique thereof—had depended. Within a span of a few years, Carl Menger published his own *Principles of Economics* (1871), William Jevons published his *Theory of Political Economy* (1871), and Léon Walras published *Éléments d'économie politique pure* (1874). The marginalist revolution was well under way, and Marx's critique of Ricardo would be quickly overshadowed. See Robert Meister, *Political Identity: Thinking Through Marx* (Cambridge, MA: Blackwell, 1990), p. 314.

3. By 2005, close to 40 percent of corporate profits in the United States were claimed by the financial sector, while manufacturing profits had dropped below 10 percent. See John Bellamy Foster and Fred Magdoff, *The Great Financial Crisis: Causes and Consequences* (New York: Monthly Review Press, 2009), p. 55, and David Harvey, *The Enigma of Capital and the Crises of Capitalism* (Oxford: Oxford University Press, 2010), p. 22. Of course, this trend may be perfectly compatible with Marx's overall framework, but not without recourse to Marx's analysis of "fictitious capital" in *Capital: A Critique of Political Economy*, vol. 3, trans. David Fernbach (London: Penguin, 1981), p. 525.

4. Martin Scorsese (dir.), *The Wolf of Wall Street* (Paramount, 2013). To be clear, it is not merely in appearance that Moneybags has changed. To quote Robyn Marasco, "the mode of reasoning we might identify with the industrial capitalist factory owner, for instance, is quite distinct from the mode of reasoning characteristic of the hedge-fund manager, the investment banker, and the Wall Street speculator." Robyn Marasco, "Neoliberalism and Governmental Reason," in Roger Berkowitz and Taun N. Toay (eds.), *The Intellectual Origins of the Global Financial Crisis* (New York: Fordham University Press, 2012), p. 161.

5. See Mary Poovey, "Stories We Tell about Liberal Markets: The Efficient Market Hypothesis and Great-Men Histories of Change," in Simon Gunn and James Vernon (eds.), *The Peculiarities of Liberal Modernity in Imperial Britain* (Berkeley: University of California Press, 2011), p. 200.

6. See Marieke de Goede, *Virtue, Fortune, and Faith: A Genealogy of Finance* (Minneapolis: University of Minnesota Press, 2005), p. 126.

7. Paul A. Samuelson, "Mathematics of Speculative Price," *SIAM Review* 15.1 (January 1973), p. 5. Cited in Peter Bernstein, *Capital Ideas: The Improbable Origins of Modern Wall Street* (New York: Free Press, 1992) and in Donald MacKenzie, *An Engine, Not a Camera: How Financial Models Shape Markets* (Cambridge, MA: MIT Press, 2006), p. 64.

8. See, in particular, Marx, *Capital*, vol. 3, pp. 459–671.

9. For the purposes of this chapter, I focus only on the world of consumer credit and mortgage markets. Analogous processes can be seen in other areas of finance, where the development of modern portfolio theory—together with the invention of the capital asset pricing model and the Black-Scholes options-pricing formula—have similarly revolutionized financial markets by allowing investors to manage the risk they once shunned, leading to an ever-increasing number of trades at ever-increasing speeds and, of course, to ever-greater financial profits.

10. Marx, *Capital*, vol. 1, p. 272.

11. *Ibid.*, p. 784.

12. Donncha Marron, *Consumer Credit in the United States: A Sociological Perspective from the Nineteenth Century to the Present* (New York: Palgrave Macmillan, 2009), pp. 49 and 118. For complementary analyses of the evolution of consumer credit in the United States in particular, see Paul Langley, *The Everyday Life of Global Finance: Saving and Borrowing in Anglo-America* (Oxford: Oxford University Press, 2009); Annie McClanahan, "Bad Credit: The Character of Credit Scoring," *Representations* 126.1 (Spring 2014), pp. 31–57; and Andrew Leyshon and Nigel Thrift, "Lists Come Alive: Electronic Systems of Knowledge and the Rise of Credit-Scoring in Retail Banking," *Economy and Society* 28.3 (August 1999), pp. 434–66.

13. David Durand, *Risk Elements in Consumer Installment Financing* (New York: National Bureau of Economic Research, 1941), cited in Marron, *Consumer Credit in the United States*, p. 120.

14. Marron, *Consumer Credit in the United States*, p. 120.

15. *Ibid.*, pp. 120–21.

16. Louis Hyman, *Borrow: The American Way of Debt* (New York: Vintage, 2012), pp. 148–79.

17. See Ian Hacking, *The Taming of Chance* (Cambridge: Cambridge University Press, 1990), p. 35, and Marron, *Consumer Credit in the United States*, p. 105.

18. I rely significantly on Martha Poon's painstaking studies of the rise of the FICO score: Martha Poon, "From New Deal Institutions to Capital Markets: Commercial Consumer Risk Scores and the Making of Subprime Mortgage Finance," *Accounting, Organizations, and Society* 34.5 (July 2009), pp. 654–74, and Poon, "Scorecards as Devices for Consumer Credit: The Case of Fair, Isaac & Company Incorporated," *Sociological Review* 55, supplement s2 (October 2007), pp. 284–306.

19. Poon, "From New Deal Institutions to Capital Markets," p. 663.

20. There have been many regulatory changes over the years that have favored banks and credit card companies in the United States, but none perhaps has been more significant than the Supreme Court's 1978 ruling in Marquette National Bank v. First of Omaha Services Corporation, which effectively led to the repeal of the McFadden Act of 1927 and the anti-usury provisions therein. Prior to 1978, banks were not allowed to charge more than 2.5 to 3 percent more than the cost incurred by making the loan. After 1978, all such restrictions were gone. See Susanne Soederberg, *Debtfare States and the Poverty Industry: Money, Discipline and the Surplus Population* (London: Routledge, 2014), pp. 84–85.

21. See Bernstein, *Capital Ideas*, pp. 41–60.

22. For a study of the changing relations between bankers and their clients in the age of disintermediation, at least in the French context, see Jeanne Lazarus, *L'épreuve de l'argent: Banques, banquiers, clients* (Paris: Calmann-Lévy, 2012).

23. David Harvey, "The Right to the City," *New Left Review* 53 (September–October 2008), p. 27.

24. The Federal National Mortgage Association would eventually be rebaptized Fannie Mae in 1968, when its status changed to that of a "government-

sponsored enterprise." For a fuller discussion of the role of the federal government in shaping and reshaping the U.S. housing market over the years, see Kevin Fox Gotham, "Creating Liquidity Out of Spatial Fixity: The Secondary Circuit of Capital and the Restructuring of the U.S. Housing Finance System," in Manuel B. Aalbers (ed.), *Subprime Cities: The Political Economy of Mortgage Markets* (Oxford: Wiley-Blackwell, 2012), pp. 25–52.

25. Poon, "From New Deal Institutions to Capital Markets," p. 660.

26. *Ibid.*

27. For many years, these government-sponsored enterprises (GSEs) had their own system—complete with letter grades—for identifying bonds as investment grade, noninvestment grade, or less than prime. But as Martha Poon explains, while lenders around the country could all use the GSE classification system when originating loans, different companies would interpret the rules in different ways, meaning that no real agreement could exist on the value or riskiness of the individual debts, let alone the pools of debts.

28. Poon, "From New Deal Institutions to Capital Markets," p. 664.

29. *Ibid.*

30. *Ibid.*, p. 665.

31. William Shakespeare, *The Merchant of Venice*, act 1, scene 3. As Marx himself puts it, "by a 'good' man, the one who bestows his trust understands, like Shylock, a man who is 'able to pay.'" Karl Marx, *Comments on James Mill*, quoted in Maurizio Lazzarato, *The Making of Indebted Man*, trans. Joshua David Jordan (Cambridge, MA: MIT Press, 2012), p. 58. For a discussion of *The Merchant of Venice* and its relevance to practices of arbitrage, see Hirokazu Miyazaki, *Arbitraging Japan: Dreams of Capitalism at the End of Finance* (Berkeley: University of California Press, 2013), pp. 26–42.

32. As Sam Jones explains in the *Financial Times*, "when mathematicians and physicists want to describe the chances of events occurring, they often rely on a curve called a copula. The Latin root is a noun meaning a 'link or tie,' and indeed, copulas connect variables in such a way that their interdependence can be plotted." The Gaussian copula, in particular (better known as a bell curve or normal distribution), made it possible to calculate the probability that

different borrowers would default at the same time: "In the same way that actu-
aries could tell their employers the chances of Johnny Cash dying soon after
June Carter without knowing anything about Cash other than the fact of his
recent widowhood, so quants could tell their employers the effect one company
defaulting might have on another doing the same—without knowing anything
about the companies themselves. From this point on, it really could be, would
be, a number-crunching game." Sam Jones, "The Formula That Felled Wall
Street," *Financial Times*, April 24, 2009. See also Donald MacKenzie and
Taylor Spears, "'The Formula That Killed Wall Street'?: The Gaussian Copula
and the Material Cultures of Modelling" (June 2012), available online at www.
sps.ed.ac.uk/__data/assets/pdf_file/0003/84243/Gaussian14.pdf.

33. In the mortgage market, as we have seen, the use of Fair, Isaac's credit
scores has been critical to the process of securitization; in the bond market,
similarly, it is the rating agencies Standard & Poor's, Moody's, and Fitch
that have taken it upon themselves to evaluate bond issuers, distinguishing
between those bonds that are "investment grade" and those that are merely
"speculative." And in the stock market, of course, traders are able to rely
on indices such as the S&P 500 to calculate the β of individual stocks and
determine what and when to sell or buy.

34. On the rise of "immaterial labor" and some of the surrounding Marxo-
logical debates regarding the category of labor more generally, see Maurizio
Lazzarato, "Immaterial Labor," trans. Paul Colilli and Ed Emery, in Paolo
Virno and Michael Hardt (eds.), *Radical Thought in Italy: A Potential Politics*
(Minneapolis: University of Minnesota Press, 1996), pp. 133–47; Michael Hardt
and Antonio Negri, *Multitude: War and Democracy in the Age of Empire* (New
York: Penguin, 2004), pp. 102–54; Ricardo Antunes, *The Meanings of Work:
Essays on the Affirmation and Negation of Work*, trans. Elizabeth Molinari (1999;
Chicago: Haymarket, 2013), pp. 96–111; and Pierre-Yves Gomez, *Le travail
invisible: Enquête sur une disparition* (Paris: Éditions François Bourin, 2013).

35. For insights into the ways that finance and liberal conceptions of freedom evolve together throughout the nineteenth century, see Pat O'Malley, *Risk,
Uncertainty and Government* (London: Routledge, 2004), pp. 77–94; Jonathan

Levy, *Freaks of Fortune: The Emerging World of Capitalism and Risk in America* (Cambridge, MA: Harvard University Press, 2012), especially chapters 3 and 4.

36. J. L. Austin, *How To Do Things with Words* (Oxford: Oxford University Press, 1962), pp. 9 and 22.

37. Marx, *Capital*, vol. 1, pp. 300–301.

38. *Ibid.*, p. 279.

39. Marx, *Capital*, vol. 3, p. 525.

40. In a somewhat different register, Dick Bryan, Michael Rafferty, and Chris Jefferis make the persuasive case that "the household creation and ongoing viability of the assets that go into ABS can be understood as a process of coproduction." This, they suggest, is "labor's production *within* finance, albeit it involves people merely paying household bills, unaware that they are building critical asset classes for securities." And though my own analysis does not draw on the work of Gilles Deleuze, it is not entirely incompatible with some of his insights. As Bryan, Rafferty, and Jefferis point out, "While Deleuze develops his analysis in relation to consumption, he provides a means to understand new forms of production in finance and processes outside the discourse of [socially necessary labor time]. Specifically, Deleuze gives us access to the way capital imagines new, distinctive securities and the way particular bundles of household payments can be evaluated for default risk." See Dick Bryan, Michael Rafferty, and Chris Jefferis, "Risk and Value: Finance, Labor, and Production," *South Atlantic Quarterly* 114.2 (April 2015), pp. 320–21.

41. "In the 1970s," as Jennifer Taub notes, "*individuals* held about 80 percent of U.S. corporate equities; however, currently, giant intermediary *institutions* hold legal title to approximately 70 percent. Also, the vast majority of outstanding corporate and government bonds are held by institutions. While institutions may hold legal title to these investments, they are not the real investors who put their money at risk. Instead, they are often investing the capital of real people whose money is funneled to them through various other intermediaries. For example, in 2009, one class of institutional investor, the mutual fund, held 24 percent of U.S. equities." Jennifer S. Taub, "The Sophisticated Investor and the Global Crisis," in James P. Hawley, Shyam J. Kamath,

and Andrew T. Williams (eds.), *Corporate Governance Failures: The Role of Institutional Investors in the Global Financial Crisis* (Philadelphia: University of Pennsylvania Press, 2011), p. 190.

42. As Robin Blackburn points out, the development of new hedging techniques has made possible "advances in the efficiency of capital but the resulting gains are disproportionately reaped by financial intermediaries, especially those with access to huge computing power and privileged information networks." See Robin Blackburn, "Finance and the Fourth Dimension," *New Left Review* 39 (May–June 2006), p. 67. See also Edward LiPuma and Benjamin Lee, *Financial Derivatives and the Globalization of Risk* (Durham, NC: Duke University Press, 2004).

43. Harry Markowitz, "Foundations of Portfolio Theory," Nobel Lecture, December 7, 1990, in Karl-Göran Mäler (ed.), *Nobel Lectures, Economics 1981– 1990* (Singapore: World Scientific Publishing, 1992), p. 279. And as Andrew Leyshon and Nigel Thrift point out, "the benefits of the discovery of new assets or classes of assets are mainly reaped by financial intermediaries, especially those with access to computing power and software which can remake assets so that they are tradeable." Andrew Leyshon and Nigel Thrift, "The Capitalization of Almost Everything: The Future of Finance and Capitalism," *Theory, Culture and Society* 24.7–8 (2007), pp. 109–110.

44. For better or worse, I have spoken of Moneybags in the singular and may have given the misleading impression that Moneybags is simply a moneylender. The truth is, the cast of characters of contemporary capitalism is quite diverse, and one of the most important parts is now played by rating agencies and their experts, whose job is to determine (in every sense of the word) the relative creditworthiness of the other players. For a general overview of rating agencies and their role, see Norbert Gaillard, *Les agences de notation* (Paris: La Découverte, 2010). For more critical analyses of the same, see Timothy Sinclair, *The New Masters of Capital: American Bond Rating Agencies and the Politics of Creditworthiness* (Ithaca, NY: Cornell University Press, 2005); Alexandra Ouroussoff, *Wall Street at War: The Secret Struggle for the Global Economy* (Cambridge: Polity, 2010); and Samuel Didier and Nicolas Weill,

Les dessous du triple A: Agences de notation: récit de l'intérieur (Paris: Omni-science, 2012).

45. Anselm Jappe, *Les aventures de la marchandise: Pour une nouvelle critique de la valeur* (Paris: Denoël, 2003), p. 119.

46. Dennis Berman, Henny Sender, and Ian McDonald, "GM Auction Won't Be Simple," *Wall Street Journal*, December 9, 2005, cited in Blackburn, "Finance and the Fourth Dimension," p. 44.

47. To be fair, the terms of the critique have always been changing, and over the years, much has been done to complicate the implausibly substantivist theory of value that so many have attributed to Marx. See, for instance, the work of Isaak I. Rubin, *Essays on Marx's Theory of Value*, trans. Miloš Samardžija and Fredy Perlman (1928; Detroit: Black and Red, 1972), and Diane Elson (ed.), *Value: The Representation of Labour in Capitalism* (London: CSE Books, 1979). Along these lines, I should acknowledge that the argument presented here—without implicating their authors in any way—owes much to the following interpretations of Marx on the question of value: Moishe Postone, *Time, Labor, and Social Domination: A Reinterpretation of Marx's Critical Theory* (Cambridge: Cambridge University Press, 1993); Jean-Marie Vincent, *Un autre Marx: Après les marxismes* (Paris: Éditions Page deux, 2001); Jappe, *Les aventures de la marchandise*; Antoine Artous, *Le fétichisme chez Marx: Le marxisme comme théorie critique* (Paris: Syllepse, 2006); Ernst Lohoff and Norbert Trenkle, *Die Große Entwertung: Warum Spekulation und Staatsverschuldung nicht die Ursache der Krise sind* (Münster: Unrast, 2012), available in French as *La grande dévalorisation: Pourquoi la spéculation et la dette de l'État ne sont pas les causes de la crise*, trans. Paul Braud, Gérard Briche, and Vincent Roulet (Paris: Post-éditions, 2014); and Eric Martin and Maxime Ouellet, eds., *La tyrannie de la valeur: Débats pour le renouvellement de la théorie critique* (Montréal: Les Éditions Écosociété, 2014).

CHAPTER FOUR: FROM VAGABOND TO SUBPRIME

1. On the change of tone in Marx's writing, see David Harvey, *A Companion to Marx's Capital* (London: Verso, 2010), p. 279. On the literary structure of

the argument more generally, see Robert Paul Wolff, *Moneybags Must Be So Lucky: On the Literary Structure of Capital* (Amherst: University of Massachusetts Press, 1988).

2. Karl Marx, *Capital: A Critique of Political Economy*, vol. 1, trans. Ben Fowkes (New York: Penguin, 1990), pp. 272 and 746.

3. *Ibid.*, p. 873

4. *Ibid.*

5. *Ibid.*, pp. 871–940. Fowkes translates *ursprüngliche Akkumulation* as "primitive accumulation." Another choice might have been "original accumulation."

6. *Ibid.*, p. 874.

7. *Ibid.*, p. 896.

8. *Ibid.*

9. David Harvey, *The New Imperialism* (Oxford: Oxford University Press, 2003), p. 137. Marx's analysis of the "so-called primitive accumulation" has been a source of inspiration for countless readers since at least Rosa Luxemburg. David Harvey's recent reinterpretation of Marx is one the most widely cited, but recent scholarship also includes Werner Bonefeld, "The Permanence of Primitive Accumulation: Commodity Fetishism and Social Constitution," *The Commoner*, no. 2 (September 2001); Jim Glassman, "Primitive Accumulation, Accumulation by Dispossession, Accumulation by 'Extra-Economic' Means," *Progress in Human Geography* 30.5 (October 2006), pp. 608–25; Jason Read, "Primitive Accumulation: The Aleatory Foundation of Capital," *Rethinking Marxism* 14.2 (Summer 2002), pp. 24–49; Silvia Federici, *Caliban and the Witch: Women, the Body, and Primitive Accumulation* (New York: Autonomedia, 2004); Massimo de Angelis, *The Beginning of History: Value Struggles and Global Capital* (London: Pluto Press, 2007); Kalyan K. Sanyal, *Rethinking Capitalist Development: Primitive Accumulation, Governmentality and Post-Colonial Capitalism* (London: Routledge, 2007); Sandro Mezzadra, "The Topicality of Prehistory: A New Reading of Marx's Analysis of 'So-called Primitive Accumulation,'" *Rethinking Marxism* 23.3 (2011), pp. 302–21; Saskia Sassen, *Expulsions: Brutality and Complexity in the Global Economy* (Cambridge,

MA: Harvard University Press, 2014); Glen Sean Coulthard, *Red Skin, White Masks: Rejecting the Colonial Politics of Recognition* (Minneapolis: University of Minnesota Press, 2014); Pierre Dardot and Christian Laval, *Commun: Essai sur la révolution au XXIe siècle* (Paris: La Découverte, 2014).

10. See Saskia Sassen, "A Savage Sorting of Winners and Losers: Contemporary Versions of Primitive Accumulation," *Globalizations* 7.1 (2010), pp. 23–50.

11. On the rise of finance after the abandonment of the Bretton Woods agreement, see Giovanni Arrighi, *The Long Twentieth Century: Money, Power, and the Origins of Our Time* (New York: Verso, 1994); for accounts of the political origins of American financialization, see Greta Krippner, *Capitalizing on Crisis: The Political Origins of the Rise of Finance* (Cambridge, MA: Harvard University Press, 2011), and Gerald Davis, *Managed by the Markets: How Finance Re-Shaped America* (Oxford: Oxford University Press, 2009).

12. The language of "dividuals" is not my own, but aptly captures some of what I am describing here. See Gilles Deleuze, *Pourparlers* (Paris: Minuit, 1990), p. 244; Maurizio Lazzarato, *The Making of Indebted Man*, trans. Joshua David Jordan (Cambridge: MIT Press, 2012), p. 148; Brian Massumi, *The Power at the End of the Economy* (Durham, NC: Duke University Press, 2014), pp. 32–35; and Arjun Appadurai, *Banking on Words: The Failure of Language in Derivative Finance* (Chicago: University of Chicago Press, 2015), pp. 101–24.

13. On debt and discipline more generally, see Tayyab Mahmud, "Debt and Discipline," *American Quarterly* 64.3 (September 2012), pp. 469–94; Ananya Roy, "Subjects of Risk: Technologies of Gender in the Making of Millennial Modernity," *Public Culture* 24.1 (2012), pp. 131–55; Mark Kear, "Governing *Homo Subprimicus*: Beyond Financial Citizenship, Exclusion, and Rights," *Antipode* 45.4 (September 2013), pp. 1–21; Paul Langley, "Equipping Entrepreneurs: Consuming Credit and Credit Scores," *Consumption Markets and Culture* 17.5 (2014), pp. 448–467.

14. Karl Marx to Arnold Ruge, September 1843, *MECW*, vol. 3, p. 142.

15. See Karl Polanyi, *The Great Transformation* (Boston: Beacon, 1944).

16. On the various forms taken by the social state in the twentieth century,

see Thomas Piketty, *Le capital au XXIe siècle* (Paris: Seuil, 2013), pp. 756–91, available in English as Thomas Piketty, *Capital in the Twenty-First Century*, trans. Arthur Goldhammer (Cambridge, MA: Belknap Press of Harvard University Press, 2014), pp. 474–92. On the French case, see François Ewald, *L'État providence* (Paris: Grasset, 1986). See also Christophe Ramaux, "Quelle théorie pour l'état social?: Apports et limites de la référence assurantielle. Relire François Ewald 20 ans après *L'État providence*," *Revue française des affaires sociales* 1.1 (2007), pp. 13–34.

17. See Gøsta Esping-Andersen, *The Three Worlds of Welfare Capitalism* (Princeton, NJ: Princeton University Press, 1990); Robert Castel, *Les métamorphoses de la question sociale: Une chronique du salariat* (Paris: Gallimard, 1999), available in English as *From Manual Workers to Wage Laborers*, ed. and trans. Richard Boyd (New Brunswick, NJ: Transaction, 2003).

18. For all its virtues, there are many reasons not to be too nostalgic for the twentieth-century welfare state: among them, the myriad exclusions that were everywhere inscribed in its social insurance policies. See Nancy Ettlinger, "Precarity Unbound," *Alternatives Global, Local, Political* 32.3 (July 2007), pp. 322–23; Isabell Lorey, *States of Insecurity* (New York: Verso, 2015), p. 57; Melinda Cooper, "Shadow Money and the Shadow Workforce: Rethinking Labor and Liquidity," *South Atlantic Quarterly* 114.2 (April 2015), pp. 401–402.

19. On the complicated relation between Keynes and White, see Benn Steil, *The Battle of Bretton Woods: John Maynard Keynes, Harry Dexter White, and the Making of a New World Order* (Princeton, NJ: Princeton University Press, 2013).

20. Geoff Mann, *Disassembly Required: A Fieldguide to Actually Existing Capitalism* (Oakland, CA: AK Press, 2013), p. 117. This chapter takes much from Mann, including the clever reference to "actually existing capitalism."

21. *Ibid.*, p. 126.

22. See Edward LiPuma and Benjamin Lee, *Financial Derivatives and the Globalization of Risk* (Durham, NC: Duke University Press, 2004); see also Dick Bryan and Michael Rafferty, *Capitalism with Derivatives: A Political Economy of Financial Derivatives, Capital and Class* (New York: Palgrave Macmillan, 2006), pp. 112–34.

23. See David Harvey, *A Brief History of Neoliberalism* (Oxford: Oxford University Press, 2005), p. 23.

24. On the relation between Volcker's policies and Ronald Reagan's assault on labor, see Martijn Konings, "State of Speculation: Contingency, Measure, and the Politics of Plastic Value," *South Atlantic Quarterly* 114.2 (April 2015), p. 267.

25. Already in 1973, as Dick Bryan, Michael Rafferty, and Chris Jefferis point out, the Italian philosopher Antonio Negri made the case that the Keynesian state had taken it upon itself to link the present to the future in various ways, for example, through the guarantee of fixed exchange rates, stable interest rates, and a minimum wage. As Negri also explained, however, this task shifted to the market in the 1970s, with the effect that by now, as Bryan, Rafferty, and Jefferis put it, the "risks of the future" have become "increasingly individualized and transferable and are thus only social in some partial, private way by conscious process of mass hedging." See Dick Bryan, Michael Rafferty, and Chris Jefferis, "Risk and Value: Finance, Labor, and Production," *South Atlantic Quarterly* 114.2 (April 2015), p. 308.

26. Jacob S. Hacker, *The Great Risk Shift* (Oxford: Oxford University Press, 2006), p. 7.

27. See Pat O'Malley, "Uncertain Subjects: Risks, Liberalism and Contract," *Economy and Society* 29.4 (2000), pp. 460–84.

28. On the injunction to "invest in the future," see Annie McClanahan, "Investing in the Future," *Journal of Cultural Economy* 6.1 (2013), pp. 78–93.

29. Jacob S. Hacker, "Statement Before the Committee on Senate Health, Education, Labor, and Pensions," January 16, 2007, available online at http://blog.oup.com/2007/01/jacob_hacker_ad.

30. Hacker writes eloquently of risk having shifted "back on to the workers and their families." While the formulation is evocative, it is worth noting that "risk" is hardly a natural category—meaning that whatever risks are now borne by "workers and their families" were not necessarily recognizable as such prior to the policy shifts that Hacker describes. For help in historicizing risk and attendant categories, see Ian Hacking, *The Emergence of Probability*

(Cambridge: Cambridge University Press, 1975); Lorenz Krüger, Lorraine J. Daston, and Michael Heidelberger, eds., *The Probabilistic Revolution, Vol. 1: Ideas in History* (Cambridge, MA: MIT Press, 1987); Mary Morgan, Lorenz Krüger, and Gerd Gigerenzer, eds., *The Probabilistic Revolution, Vol. 2: Ideas in the Sciences* (Cambridge, MA: MIT Press, 1987); Gerd Gigerenzer et al., *The Empire of Chance: How Probability Changed Science and Everyday Life* (Cambridge: Cambridge University Press, 1989); Ian Hacking, *The Taming of Chance* (Cambridge: Cambridge University Press, 1990); François Ewald, "Insurance and Risk," and Robert Castel, "From Dangerousness to Risk," in Graham Burchell, Colin Gordon, and Peter Miller (eds.), *The Foucault Effect: Studies in Governmentality* (Chicago: University of Chicago Press, 1991), pp. 197–211 and 281–98; Ulrich Beck, *Risk Society: Towards a New Modernity* (London: Sage, 1992); Peter Bernstein, *Against the Gods: The Remarkable Story of Risk* (New York: John Wiley and Sons, 1996); Mitchell Dean, "Risk, Calculable and Incalculable," *Soziale Welt* 49.1 (1998), pp. 25–42; Tom Baker and Jonathan Simon (eds.), *Embracing Risk: The Changing Culture of Insurance and Responsibility* (Chicago: University of Chicago Press, 2002); Pat O'Malley, *Risk, Uncertainty and Government* (London: Routledge, 2004); Bernard Harcourt, *Against Prediction: Punishing and Policing in an Actuarial Age* (Chicago: University of Chicago Press, 2007); Nicolas Bouleau, *Risk and Meaning: Adversaries in Art, Science and Philosophy*, trans. Dené Oglesby and Martin Crossley (Berlin: Springer, 2011); Frédéric Gros, *Le principe sécurité* (Paris: Gallimard, 2012); Jonathan Levy, *Freaks of Fortune: The Emerging World of Capitalism and Risk in America* (Cambridge, MA: Harvard University Press, 2012); Louise Amoore, *The Politics of Possibility: Risk and Security Beyond Probability* (Durham, NC: Duke University Press, 2013), pp. 29–78.

31. Hacker, *The Great Risk Shift*, p. 14.

32. On the vulnerability of senior citizens, in particular, see Johnna Montgomerie, "America's Debt-Safety Net," *Public Administration* 91.4, pp. 881–85.

33. On the changes to the tax code and the subsequent rise of pension funds, see Davis, *Managed by the Markets*, p. 132. I focus here on the case of the United States, but similar trends may also be observed elsewhere. See, for

instance, Hadas Weiss, "Financialization and Its Discontents: Israelis Negotiating Pensions," *American Anthropologist,* July 14, 2015, available at http://dx.doi.org/10.1111/aman.12283.

34. Max Haiven, "Walmart, Financialization, and the Cultural Politics of Securitization," *Cultural Politics* 9.3 (2013), p. 245.

35. See, for instance, Susanne Soederberg, *Debtfare States and the Poverty Industry: Money, Discipline and the Surplus Population* (London: Routledge, 2014) and David Harvey, *The Enigma of Capital and the Crises of Capitalism* (Oxford: Oxford University Press, 2010), p. 17.

36. Marx, *Capital,* vol. 1, p. 876.

37. Unlike value, which famously "does not have its description branded on its forehead," the enslaved vagabond under Henry VI, if he is "absent for a fortnight," is liable to be "condemned to slavery for life" and to be "branded on forehead or back with the letter S; if he runs away three times, he is to be executed as a felon." *Ibid.,* pp. 167 and 897.

38. As Lazzarato puts it, "The creditor's power over the debtor very much resembles Foucault's last definition of power: an action carried out on another action, an action that keeps the person over which power is exercised 'free.' The power of debt leaves you free, and it encourages you and pushes you to act in such a way that you are able to honor your debts (even if, like the IMF, it has a tendency to devour 'debtors' by imposing economic policies that promote 'recession')." Lazzarato, *The Making of Indebted Man,* p. 31.

39. Natalie Kitroeff, "Young and in Debt in New York City," *New York Times,* June 6, 2014. Public schools are not what they used to be. In 1995, yearly instate tuition and fees at the University of Washington amounted to $3,019 per year, or roughly 12 percent of the average yearly income in that state, according to the figures available from the University of Washington and the U.S. Bureau of Economic Analysis. By 2013, the cost of a year's worth of education had reached $12,397, or 26 percent of the average yearly income, leaving most students no choice but to borrow. For more on the development of the student loan industry in the United States, see Soederberg, *Debtfare States and the Poverty Industry,* pp. 104–32.

40. The fact that many students remain partly dependent on their parents would seem to make them particularly attractive to lenders. According to Johnna Montgomerie, "Industry reports claim it is students' household resources, specifically parental income and access to student loans, which make them suitable risks against default." See Johnna Montgomerie, "Spectre of the Subprime Borrower—Beyond a Credit Score Perspective," CRESC Working Paper Series Working Paper no. 58, p. 13, available at http://www.cresc.ac.uk/medialibrary/workingpapers/wp58.pdf.

41. See Paul Kiel, "The Great American Foreclosure Story: The Struggle for Justice and a Place to Call Home," *Propublica*, April 10, 2012.

42. For an account of how "human capital theory" might help explain and address lingering concerns over the "gender gap" in pay, see Gary S. Becker, "The Economic Way of Looking at Life," Nobel Lecture, December 9, 1992, in Torsten Persson (ed.), *Nobel Lectures, Economics 1991–1995* (Singapore: World Scientific Publishing, 1997), p. 45.

43. See Charles Duhigg, "What Does Your Credit-Card Company Know About You," *New York Times Magazine*, May 12, 2009.

44. Specifically, the Equal Credit Opportunities Act of 1974 outlaws discrimination based on the gender, marital status, race, religion, national origin, or source of income of the applicant.

45. For a discussion of the various ways in which lenders and credit rating agencies are able to discriminate among borrowers, see Martha Poon, "Statistically Discriminating Without Discrimination," Centre de Sociologie des Organisations, available at http://www.ardis-recherche.fr/files/downloads_file_31.pdf. See also Marion Fourcade and Kieran Healy, "Classification Situations: Life-Chances in the Neoliberal Era," *Accounting, Organizations and Society* 38.8 (2013), pp. 559–72; Stephen Ross and John Yinger, *The Color of Credit: Mortgage Discrimination, Research Methodology, and Fair Lending Enforcement* (Cambridge, MA: MIT Press, 2002); and Danielle Keats Citron and Frank Pasquale, "The Scored Society: Due Process for Automated Predictions," *Washington Law Review* 89.1 (March 2014), pp. 1–33. On the racialized parameters of the subprime crisis, see Gary A. Dymski, "Racial Exclusion

and the Political Economy of the Subprime Crisis," *Historical Materialism* 17.2 (2009), pp. 149–79; Angie K. Beeman, Davita Silfen Glasberg, and Colleen Casey, "Whiteness as Property: Predatory Lending and the Reproduction of Racialized Inequality," *Critical Sociology* 37.1 (2010), pp. 27–46.

46. It is perhaps unsurprising, then, that as Susanne Soederberg reports, the "demographics of personal bankruptcies represent those groups and classes that were most vulnerable prior to entering into a contract with credit cards and other forms of consumer debt." In the United States, "African-American and Latino workers are 500 percent more likely than white homeowners to find themselves in bankruptcy. Other groups likely to file for bankruptcy are laid-off workers, whose numbers are rising; and older Americans, who are now the fastest-growing age group in bankruptcy." Soederberg, *Debtfare States and the Poverty Industry*, p. 87.

47. See, among others, Johnna Montgomerie "The Financialization of the American Credit Card Industry," *Competition and Change* 10.3 (September 2006), pp. 301–19.

48. As Susanne Soederberg documents, those whose incomes (or lack thereof) leave them most vulnerable have been turning to credit cards in great numbers. Thus, from 1989 to 2001, she reports (citing figures provided by Demos in 2003), "credit card debt among low-income families grew by an astonishing 184 percent," while personal bankruptcies—and this, despite the Bankruptcy Reform Act of 1978—"continued to rise alongside poverty rates, unemployment rates and interest rates." As Soederberg further explains, it is widely understood that "a key cause" of these personal bankruptcies is the fact that workers have become "dependent" on this revolving credit card debt to help finance basic subsistence needs during hard economic times. Soederberg, *Debtfare States and the Poverty Industry*, p. 87.

49. Marx, *Capital*, vol. 1, p. 178.

50. As Lazzarato points out, we maintain through consumption "an unwitting relationship with the debt economy. We carry within us the creditor-debtor relation in our pockets and wallets, encoded in the magnetic strip on our credit cards. Indeed, this little strip of plastic hides two seemingly harmless

operations: the *automatic* institution of the credit relation, which thereby establishes *permanent* debt. The credit card is the simplest way to transform its owner into a permanent debtor, an 'indebted man' for life." Lazzarato, *The Making of Indebted Man*, p. 20.

51. For a description of "What You Need to Know About Credit Card Processing," see Paul Downs's post by the same title on the *New York Times* Web site, March 25, 2013, http://boss.blogs.nytimes.com/2013/03/25.

52. See Michel Feher, "Self-Appreciation; or, The Aspirations of Human Capital," *Public Culture* 21.1 (2009).

53. Adam Smith, *An Inquiry into the Nature and Causes of the Wealth of Nations* (1776; Chicago: University of Chicago Press, 1976), p. 17.

54. Polanyi, *The Great Transformation*, pp. 68–76.

55. Michel Feher, "Self-Appreciation," p. 31. On "investment as a neoliberal technology of self," see also Paul Langley, "Uncertain Subjects of Anglo-American Financialization," *Cultural Critique* 65 (Fall 2007), pp. 67–91.

56. On the changing morphology of *Homo œconomicus* and the rise of the "entrepreneur of the self," see Michel Foucault, *The Birth of Biopolitics: Lectures at the Collège de France, 1978–1979*, trans. Graham Burchell (New York: Palgrave Macmillan, 2008); Thomas Lemke, "'The Birth of Bio-Politics': Michel Foucault's Lecture at the Collège de France on Neo-Liberal Governmentality," *Economy and Society* 30.2 (2001), pp. 190–207; Wendy Brown, *Edgework: Critical Essays on Knowledge and Politics* (Princeton, NJ: Princeton University Press, 2005); Christian Laval, *L'homme économique: Essai sur les racines du néolibéralisme* (Paris: Gallimard, 2007); Jason Read, "A Genealogy of Homo-Economicus: Neoliberalism and the Production of Subjectivity," *Foucault Studies* no. 6 (February 2009), pp. 25–36; and Angela Mitropoulos, *Contract and Contagion: From Biopolitics to Oikonomia* (Wivenhoe, UK: Minor Compositions, 2012), pp. 148–52.

57. Marx, *Capital*, vol. 1, p. 899. Pierre Le Pesant de Boisguilbert, *Mémoires*, in *Correspondance des contrôleurs généraux des finances*, edition of 1874, vol. 2, p. 531, quoted in Castel, *From Manual Workers to Wage Laborers*, p. 88. On the continued pertinence of the notion of a "debtors' prison," see Genevieve

LeBaron and Adrienne Roberts, "Confining Social Insecurity: Neoliberalism and the Rise of the 21st Century Debtors' Prison," *Politics and Gender* 8 (2012), pp. 25–49.

CHAPTER FIVE: WHEN GOLDMAN BROKE THE LAW

1. Francesco Guerrera, Henny Sender, and Justin Baer, "Goldman Sachs Settles with SEC," *Financial Times*, July 16, 2010.

2. Fabrice Tourre to Marine Serres, e-mail dated January 23, 2007, "Les mails étonnants de Fabrice Tourre," *L'Express*, L'Expansion.com, April 26, 2010, available at http://lexpansion.lexpress.fr/entreprises/les-mails-etonnants-de-fabrice-tourre_1449864.html.

3. See Matthew Goldstein, "Goldman's Timberwolf Deal Leads to Much Howling," Reuters, April 27, 2010, available at http://www.reuters.com/article/2010/04/27/us-goldman-twolf-idUSTRE63Q5C320100427. Matt Taibbi, to be fair, did not attack only Goldman Sachs; he took on other players as well. See Matt Taibbi, *Griftopia: A Story of Bankers, Politicians, and the Most Audacious Power Grab in American History* (New York: Spiegel and Grau, 2011).

4. According to figures released by the New York State comptroller in March 2015, Wall Street disbursed $28.5 billion in 2014 alone, divided among 167,800 employees. This was more than twice the annual earnings of all full-time minimum-wage employees in the United States, which totaled $14 billion for the same year. See Sarah Anderson, "Off the Deep End: The Wall Street Bonus Pool and Low-Wage Workers," Institute for Policy Studies, available at http://www.ips-dc.org/deep-end-wall-street, March 11, 2015. On the connection between the crisis of 2008 and the European sovereign debt crisis, see François Chesnais, *Les dettes illégitimes: Quand les banques font main basse sur les politiques publiques* (Paris: Liber Raisons d'agir, 2011). For an analysis of both the origins of public and private debt and the long-term prospects of capitalist democracy, see Wolfgang Streeck, *Buying Time: The Delayed Crisis of Democratic Capitalism* (London: Verso, 2014), especially chapters 2 and 4.

5. Marieke de Goede, "Speculative Values and Courtroom Contestations," *South Atlantic Quarterly* 114.2 (April 2015), pp. 356–57.

6. *SEC v. Fabrice Tourre*, 2010, No. 10-CV-3229, S.D. N.Y., "Amended Complaint," §6, available at https://www.sec.gov/litigation/complaints/2010/comp-pr2010-59.pdf.

7. *Ibid.*, §23.

8. *Ibid.*, §1.

9. *Testimony of Fabrice Tourre Before the Permanent Subcommittee on Investigations*, April 27, 2010, p. 1, available at http://online.wsj.com/public/resources/documents/GSTourre042710.pdf.

10. *Ibid.*

11. See John Arlidge, "'I'm Doing 'God's Work': Meet Mr. Goldman Sachs," *Sunday Times*, November 8, 2009. Fabrice Tourre to Marine Serres, e-mail dated January 23, 2007.

12. *Testimony of Fabrice Tourre Before the Permanent Subcommittee on Investigations*, April 27, 2010, pp. 1–2.

13. De Goede, "Speculative Values and Courtroom Contestations," p. 368.

14. See the expert witness report of Dwight M. Jaffee, Ph.D., "Report on Collateralized Debt Obligations (CDO) with Regard to *SEC v. Tourre*, 10-cv-3229," December 12, 2012. For a detailed study of differential remuneration within (French) investment banks, see Olivier Godechot, *Working Rich* (Paris: La Découverte, 2007).

15. *SEC v. Tourre*, §19.

16. Goldman Sachs internal e-mail, dated February 7, 2007, cited in *SEC v. Tourre*, §23.

17. See U.S. Securities and Exchange Commission, "The Investor's Advocate: How the SEC Protects Investors, Maintains Market Integrity, and Facilitates Capital Formation," http://www.sec.gov/about/whatwedo.shtml.

18. See Nathan Schuur, "Fraud Is Already Illegal: Applying Section 621 of the Dodd-Frank Act to Securities Law," *University of Michigan Journal of Law Reform* 48.2 (2015), pp. 101–32.

19. Frank J. Fabozzi and Vinod Kothari, *Introduction to Securitization* (Hoboken, NJ: Wiley and Sons, 2008), p. 15.

20. *Testimony of Fabrice Tourre Before the Permanent Subcommittee on Investigations*, April 27, 2010, p. 2.

21. Jaffee, "Report on Collateralized Debt Obligations," §30.

22. See Lynn Stout, "Why We Need Derivatives Regulation," *New York Times*, October 10, 2009.

23. Provided that someone else is willing to take the other side of the bet, a synthetic CDO can in principle be arranged without any new mortgages having to be issued. Indeed, the same mortgages can be referenced in any number of swaps, thereby only increasing the chance that defaults will prove catastrophic on a systemic level.

24. Neal Deckant, "Criticisms of Collateralized Debt Obligations in the Wake of the Goldman Sachs Scandal," *Review of Banking and Financial Law* 30.1 (2010–2011), p. 417.

25. As Melinda Cooper notes, moreover, the seller of protection in a credit default swap is "under no obligation to calculate the actuarial probability of the event in question (in this case, default) much less provide for adequate reserves, while the buyer of protection need not have any 'insurable interest' in the protected asset." Melinda Cooper, "Shadow Money and the Shadow Work-force: Rethinking Labor and Liquidity," *South Atlantic Quarterly* 114.2 (April 2015), p. 397. See also William H. Janeway, *Doing Capitalism in the Innovation Economy: Markets, Speculation and the State* (Cambridge: Cambridge University Press, 2012), p. 164.

26. See Max Weber, *The Protestant Ethic and the "Spirit" of Capitalism*, trans. Peter Baehr and Gordon C. Wells (1905; London: Penguin, 2002).

27. Writes Keynes: "Speculators may do no harm as bubbles on a steady stream of enterprise. But the position is serious when enterprise becomes the bubble on a whirlpool of speculation. When the capital development of a country becomes a by-product of the activities of a casino, the job is likely to be ill-done. The measure of success attained by Wall Street, regarded as an institution of which the proper social purpose is to direct new investment into the most profitable channels in terms of future yield, cannot be claimed as one of the outstanding triumphs of laissez-faire capitalism." John Maynard

Keynes, *The General Theory of Employment, Interest, and Money* (New York: Harcourt, 1936), p. 159.

28. See Susan Strange, *Casino Capitalism* (1986; Manchester: Manchester University Press, 1997), and Hans-Werner Sinn, *Casino Capitalism* (Oxford: Oxford University Press, 2010). Even Michel Serres, who is well known for choosing his words carefully, is said to have declared: "The financial crisis of the stock market's casino, but it's shit!" See Michel Serres, *La dépêche du midi*, October 24, 2012, available at http://www.ladepeche.fr/article/2012/10/24/ 1473223-agen-michel-serres-invite-de-la-redaction.html.

29. Of course, the experience of gambling in a casino is no less embedded in a complex set of relations and technologies than is the experience of horse betting, but it takes painstaking ethnographic work to properly document this. See Natasha Dow Schüll, *Addiction by Design: Machine Gambling in Las Vegas* (Princeton, NJ: Princeton University Press, 2014). It is easier simply to reminisce about one's grandfather's weekend habits. For an anthropological study of racing culture in both the United Kingdom and the United States, see Rebecca Cassidy, *Horse People: Thoroughbred Culture in Lexington and Newmarket* (Baltimore: Johns Hopkins University Press, 2007).

30. As Sinn puts it, it was not only Wall Street that "succumbed to gambling. Main Street did too." See Sinn, *Casino Capitalism*, p. 94.

31. On the importance of responsibility and "responsibilization" as a "social policy," see the work of Wendy Brown, who notes that "responsibilization tasks the worker, student, consumer, or indigent person with discerning and undertaking the correct strategies of self-investment and entrepreneurship for thriving and surviving; it is in this regard a manifestation of human capitalization." Wendy Brown, *Undoing the Demos: Neoliberalism's Stealth Revolution* (New York: Zone Books, 2015), pp. 132–33.

32. As Andrew Leyshon and Nigel Thrift put it in a different context, "What made the mining of these new seams of financial value apparently possible is the development of computer software that enables individuals to be assessed, sorted and aggregated along dimensions of risk and reward. The application of such techniques meant that borrowers who were once considered so risky

that they did not constitute viable assets for the retail system to be able to record on a banking balance sheet were now transformed into high-risk but high-reward income streams that, through the process of securitization, were attractive for investors looking to develop a balanced portfolio." Andrew Leyshon and Nigel Thrift, "The Capitalization of Almost Everything: The Future of Finance and Capitalism," *Theory, Culture and Society* 24.7–8 (2007), p. 108.

33. As Randy Martin points out, "risk is not unilateral but operates as a kind of moral binary, sorting out the good from the bad on the basis of capacities to contribute. The prototype financial instruments and regulatory mechanisms were introduced in the 1970s for the life of risk that would rise in the 1980s. Those who cannot manage themselves, those unable to live by risk, are considered 'at risk.'" Randy Martin, *An Empire of Indifference: American War and the Financial Logic of Risk Management* (Durham, NC: Duke University Press, 2007), p. 37.

34. Karl Marx, *Capital: A Critique of Political Economy*, vol. 1, trans. Ben Fowkes (New York: Penguin, 1990), p. 342.

35. Much has been written on Marx and vampires, and I have benefitted particularly from Franco Moretti, *Signs Taken for Wonders* (London: Verso, 1983); Chris Baldick, *In Frankenstein's Shadow: Myth, Monstrosity and Nineteenth-Century Writing* (Oxford: Clarendon Press of Oxford University Press, 1987), pp. 121–40; Mark Neocleous, "The Political Economy of the Dead: Marx's Vampires," *History of Political Thought*, 24.4 (2003), pp. 668–84; David McNally, *Monsters of the Market: Zombies, Vampires and Global Capitalism* (Leiden: Brill, 2011). On zombies and contemporary capitalism, see Jean Comaroff and John Comaroff, "Alien-Nation: Zombies, Immigrants, and Millennial Capitalism," *South Atlantic Quarterly* 101.4 (Fall 2002); Steve Shaviro, "Capitalist Monsters," *Historical Materialism* 10.4 (2002), pp. 281–90; Annalee Newitz, *Pretend We're Dead: Capitalist Monsters in American Pop Culture* (Durham, NC: Duke University Press, 2006); Sarah Juliet Lauro and Karen Embry, "A Zombie Manifesto: The Nonhuman Condition in the Era of Advanced Capitalism," *boundary 2* 35.1 (2008), pp. 85–108; Christopher M. Moreman and Cory James Rushton, eds., *Race, Oppression and the Zombie:*

Essays on Cross-Cultural Appropriations of the Caribbean Tradition (Jefferson, NC: McFarland, 2011); and Henry A. Giroux, *Zombie Politics and Culture in the Age of Casino Capitalism* (New York: Peter Lang, 2011).

36. The most famous vampire story is, of course, Bram Stoker's *Dracula*, which saw the light of day (horrors!) only in 1897, by which point Marx himself was in a coffin of his own. It does seem at least plausible, however, that Marx might have been acquainted with the Baron Azzo von Klatka, also a vampire and also a resident of Transylvania. See Karl von Wachsmann, "The Mysterious Stranger," in Mike Ashley (ed.), *Vampires: Classic Tales* (Mineola, NY: Dover Publications, 2011), pp. 33–69. What Marx may have thought of Wachsmann is another matter, but it is clear what Engels thought of him. As he put it in an attempted tragicomedy,

> He also is of noble blood
> The "C" of Wachsmann—a big one, mind—
> His equal would be hard to find.
> There's not a single almanac
> In which he hasn't left his tracks.
> Composing tales at breathless pace
> He flings them in the public's face.
> A man of sweated toil is he,
> He hasn't done a thing for verse,
> But thanks to him, as most agree,
> The public's taste was never worse.
> (Friedrich Engels, *MECW*, vol. 47, p. 432)

37. I am tempted to say, too, that while the vampire was at least a subject brimming with desire, lusting after the body and blood of his potential victims, the zombie seems closer to a figure of pure drive. Its compulsion is of another sort, and its violence—like that of financialization—would seem to undo any conventional distinction between the subject and its object. On the distinction between desire and drive as it pertains to political economy and growth, see both Jodi Dean, "Still Dancing: Drive as a Category of Political Economy,"

International Journal of Žižek Studies 6.1 (2012), and Ole Bjerg, *The Parallax of Growth: The Philosophy of Ecology and Economy* (Cambridge: Polity, 2016).

38. Fabrice Tourre to Fatiha Boukhtouche, e-mail dated January 29, 2007, "Les mails étonnants de Fabrice Tourre," *L'Express*, L'Expansion.com, April 26, 2010. For a textbook account of how to "price" a CDO (or in the monstrous Franglais used by Tourre, how to "pricer" a CDO), see C. C. Mounfield, *Synthetic CDOs: Modelling, Valuation and Risk Management* (Cambridge: Cambridge University Press, 2009), pp. 114–18. For an anthropologically informed analysis of the same, see Vincent Antonin Lépinay, *Codes of Finance: Engineering Derivatives in a Global Bank* (Princeton, NJ: Princeton University Press, 2011), pp. 75–76.

39. Fabrice Tourre to Fatiha Boukhtouche, e-mail dated January 29, 2007.

Index

Health insurance, 94.
Hedging value, 27–28, 36–41, 44–45, 60, 150 n.14; efficiency and, 39–40, 151 n.16; options pricing and, 47–50, 152 n.24.
Hollande, François, 9, 133 n.3.
Homo œconomicus, 123, 172 n.56.
Homo probabilis. See Probable man.

IKB DEUTSCHE INDUSTRIEBANK AG (IKB), 112–13, 116–17, 122.
Interest rates, 72–73, 158 n.20.
Intermediary institutions, 81, 161–62 nn.41–44.
International Monetary Fund (IMF), 91.
International monetary system, 12, 136 n.12.
Investor-borrower dynamic, 26–27.
It's a Wonderful Life (Capra), 69.

JAPPE, ANSELM, 82, 163 n.47.
J. P. Morgan, 33, 36, 142–43 n.15, 149 n.3
JPMorgan Chase & Co., 81, 149 n.3

KEYNES, JOHN MAYNARD, 91, 121, 147–48 n.30, 175 n.27. *See also* Bretton Woods monetary system.
Keynesian state, 88–93, 167 n.25.

LABOR. *See* Commodification of labor; Organized labor; Working classes.
Lehman Brothers, 20.
Levin, Carl, 110.
Lion King, The (Disney), 156 n.24.
Locke, John, 106.
Long-Term Capital Management, 143 n.17.

MANIFESTO OF THE COMMUNIST PARTY, THE (Marx and Engels), 147 n.29.
Mann, Geoff, 91, 147 n.30.
Margin Call (Chandor), 123.

Markowitz, Harry, 79; on control of the means of prediction, 81; theory of portfolio selection of, 11–14, 41–45.
Marron, Donncha, 69–71.
Marx, Karl, 10, 23–30, 145 n.23; bee architect analogy of, 24–25, 147 n.27; on capitalist societies, 33–35, 109, 149 n.6; on circulation and exchange, 82; on class, 26–27, 147 n.29; on commodification of labor power, 26–29, 34–35, 63–65, 82–84; on commodities and the nature of value, 35–41, 43–46, 50, 51, 63, 156 n.2; on crises of capitalism, 22–23; critique of contemporary finance by, 23–30, 85, 145 n.23, 148 n.34, 148 n.36; on the emergence of the working class, 85–88, 96–97, 105, 159 n.37, 169 n.37; on fetishism of financial markets, 28, 35, 51–61, 154 n.35; on forward-looking tendency of humans, 24, 145 n.24; on money as the universal equivalent, 46, 50; Moneybags character of, 28–29, 63–84, 148 n.36, 162 n.44; on political economy and the state, 14–15, 27, 89, 136 n.12, 139 n.21, 149 n.6; on power, 10; on primitive accumulation, 86–87, 164 n.9; on a single social labor force, 58–61; vampire analogy of, 124–25, 178 n.36.
Marx quotations (from *Capital*): on the association of free men, 59; on capitalist societies, 33, 109; on dependent social relations, 56; on guardians of commodities, 102–103; on history of the working class, 96–97, 169 n.37; on labor power, 43, 44, 45, 68, 79; on money, 46; on the nature of value, 37, 40, 51; on the spider and the bee, 25; on vampires, 124.
Maurer, Bill, 48.

McFadden Act of 1924, 158 n.20.

Medical insurance, 94.

Medieval European social orders, 56–58.

Meister, Robert, 139 n.21.

Merton, Robert, 47, 143 n.17. *See also* Black-Scholes-Merton model of options pricing.

Miller, Merton, 139 n.21, 153 n.31

Modern portfolio theory, 11–14, 41–45; consumer credit and, 69–73, 75, 95, 157 n.9; control of the means of prediction an, 29–30, 81; mortgage-backed securities and, 73–77, 157 n.9; pooling and assembling of portfolios and, 73, 76–81.

Money, 46, 50.

Moneybags, 28–29, 63–84, 148 n.36, 162 n.44; labor power and, 63–65, 77, 79–80; lending and risktaking by, 66–83.

Moody's, 75, 160 n.33.

Morgan, John Pierpont, 31–32.

Mortgage-backed securities, 73–77, 111–15, 157 n.9.

Mortgage crisis. *See* Subprime mortgage crisis of 2008.

Museum of American Finance, 31–32.

Mutual funds, 161 n.41.

NEOLIBERALISM, 23, 88–89; enclosed market of, 88–89, 94–96, 101–107; *Homo œconomicus* of, 123, 172 n.56; insecure subjects of, 26–27, 78, 87–89, 96–97, 106–107, 169 nn.37–38. *See also* Probable man

New York Stock Exchange (NYSE), 32–33.

Nietzsche, Friedrich, 78.

Nixon, Richard, 49–50, 92.

Nobel Prize in Economics, 13, 47, 65.

North Atlantic capitalism. *See* Anglo-American capitalism.

OLD-AGE INSURANCE, 94–95. *See also* Pension funds.

Options, 12, 47–50; assessing value of, 47–48, 152 n.24; Black-Scholes-Merton pricing model of, 12–13, 48–50, 60, 137 n.13, 139 n.21, 151 n.23, 152 n.26, 153 n.31.

Organized labor: bargains with capitalists of, 90–93; capitalist dismantling of, 15, 22–23, 95.

PASCAL, BLAISE, 55.

Paulson, John, 111–15, 122.

Pension funds, 62, 81, 84, 88, 94–95, 121–22, 168 n.33.

Personal bankruptcies, 102, 171 n.46, 171 n.48.

Personal Responsibility and Work Opportunity Act of 1996, 145–46 n.24.

Piketty, Thomas, 29, 147 n.30.

Polanyi, Karl, 89, 105.

Poon, Martha, 75, 158 n.18, 159 n.27.

Portfolio society. *See* Securitized capitalist relations.

Portfolio theory. *See* Modern portfolio theory.

Postone, Moishe, 84, 163 n.47.

Precarity, 26–27.

Predicting risk, 63–84; assessing creditworthiness in, 68–71; control of the means of prediction and, 29–30, 81; credit scores and, 71–73, 75, 97–100, 170 n.44, 171 n.46; lending algorithms in, 70–71, 75–76, 81; mortgage-backed securities and, 73–77, 157 n.9; pooling and assembling of portfolios and, 73, 76–81; rating agencies and, 52, 75, 81, 153 n.33, 160 n.33.

"The Pricing of Options and Corporate Liabilities" (Black and Scholes), 48–49.

Private insurance, 101.
Probable man (*Homo probabilis*),
85–107; credit cards of, 101–105, 171
n.48, 171 n.50; demise of the welfare state and, 88–93, 96, 145–46
n.24, 166 n.18; easy credit of,
95–100; enclosed markets of,
88–89, 94–96, 101–107; individualized risk of, 93–95, 167 n.25, 167
n.30, 176–77 nn.31–33; as insecure
neoliberal subjects, 26–27, 78,
87–89, 96–97, 106–107, 169
nn.37–38; personal indebtedness
and bankruptcies of, 102, 171 n.46,
171 n.48; risk profiles of, 99–100;
subprime borrowing by, 97–100,
121–24, 170 n.44, 171 n.46.
Proletarians. *See* Working classes.

QUANTITATIVE FINANCE ANALYSTS,
9, 17–23, 140 n.2; Frankenstein
trope of, 143 n.17; inventive
products of, 142–43 n.15.
Quantitative measures of risk. *See*
Predicting risk.

RACETRACK CAPITALISM, 121–24,
176 n.29.
Rating agencies, 52, 75, 81, 153 n.33,
160 n.33.
Reagan, Ronald, 93.
Recession of 2008. *See* Subprime
mortgage crisis of 2008.
Regulation. *See* State regulation of
financial markets.
Residential mortgage-backed securities
(RMBSs), 111–20.
Responsibilization, 176 n.31.
Retirement plans. *See* Pension funds.
Revolving credit, 95, 171 n.48.
Ricardo, David, 34, 156 n.2.
Risk: buying and selling of, 14, 66–67;
fetishizing of, 51–61, 154 n.35;

individualization of, 93–95, 167
n.25, 167 n.30, 172 n.56, 176–77
nn.31–33; prediction of, 66–84;
risk profiles of subprime borrowers,
99–100; social character of, 45–50,
56, 155 n.44.
Risk society, 45–50, 56, 155 n.44. *See
also* Securitized capitalist relations.
Robinson Crusoe (Defoe), 53–59,
154 n.37.
Rolling Stone, 9.

SAMUELSON, PAUL, 65–66.
Sassen, Saskia, 87.
Scholes, Myron, 47–49. *See also*
Black-Scholes-Merton model of
options pricing.
*Securities and Exchange Commission
v. Goldman, Sachs & Co. and Fabrice
Tourre*, 109–17.
Securitization (definition), 135 n.8.
Securitized capitalist relations (portfolio society), 10–15, 23, 31–62,
66–67, 134–35 nn.7–9; Black-
Scholes-Merton model of options
pricing in, 12–13, 48–50, 60, 137
n.13, 139 n.21, 151 n.23, 152 n.26, 153
n.31; buying and selling of risk in,
14, 66–67; computer technology in,
176 n.32; in consumer finance,
69–73, 80, 157 n.9, 158 n.20, 160
n.33, 161 n.40; control of the means
of prediction in, 29–30, 81; tranches
in, 18; efficient market hypothesis
of, 65–66; fetishizing of future risk
in, 51–61, 154 n.35; financial derivatives in, 18, 22, 25–26, 46, 60; hedging value in, 27–28, 36–41, 44–45,
150 n.14; insecure neoliberal subjects of, 78, 87–89, 96–97, 106–
107, 169 nn.37–38; intermediary
institutions of, 81, 161–62 nn.41–
44; modern portfolio theory in,

11–14, 41–45; mortgage-backed securities and, 73–77, 157 n.9; options in, 47–50; prediction of risk in, 66–84; presumed egalitarianism of, 123; probable man and subprime borrowers in, 85–107, 121–24, 170 n.44, 170 n.46; rating agencies in, 52, 75, 81, 153 n.33, 160 n.33; social character of risk in, 45–50, 56, 155 n.44; use value in, 35–38, 63. *See also* Subprime mortgage crisis of 2008.

Sharpe, William, 12–14, 42–45, 136 n.11.

Shylock (Shakespeare character), 76, 149 n.31.

Smith, Adam, 149 n.6; on the equitability and efficiency of markets, 65; on *Homo œconomicus*, 123, 172 n.56; on labor as the source of value, 15, 34; on the origins of capitalism, 85, 105.

Social security, 94–95.

Speculative value. *See* Hedging value.

Standard & Poor's, 75, 160 n.33.

State regulation of financial markets, 12–13, 18, 136 n.12; on consumer interest rates, 158 n.20; repeals of, 13, 22, 29, 140 n.3.

Steinbeck, John, 17, 20.

Stewart, Jimmy, 69.

Store credit, 69–70.

Structured finance, 18.

Student loans, 97–98, 169–70 nn.39–40.

Subprime borrowers, 97–100; credit scores and, 97–99, 170 n.44, 171 n.46; gambling analogies of, 121–24, 176–77 nn.31–33, 176 nn.28–29; higher interest rates for, 99–100; personal indebtedness and bankruptcies of, 18–20, 102, 171 n.46, 171 n.48. *See also* Probable man.

Subprime mortgage crisis of 2008, 10–11, 13, 18–30, 133 n.6; ABACUS trial and, 109–17; bank failures of, 21; delinquency and defaults in, 18–20, 102, 171 n.46, 171 n.48; distressed trading in, 20; fines paid for, 109–10; government bailouts of financial markets in, 20–21; Marxist analysis of, 22–30; power of Wall Street institutions and, 20–21, 141 n.14; quantitative finance experts and, 9, 17–23, 140 n.2, 142–43 n.15, 143 n.17; synthetic CDOs in, 112–20, 175 n.23, 175 n.25; total losses associated with, 20, 110, 141 n.4; Tourre's role in, 17–20, 22–23, 111–15, 140 n.2.

Synthetic CDOs, 112–20, 175 n.23, 175 n.25.

TAIBBI, MATT, 110, 125.

Tett, Gillian, 19–20, 142–43 n.15.

Thatcher, Margaret, 29–30, 93.

Theory of portfolio selection. *See* Modern portfolio theory.

Tourre, Fabrice, 17–20, 22–23, 140 n.2, 143 n.17; on his monstrous creations, 19–20, 110, 126–27; as scapegoat, 110–11; on synthetic CDOs, 119; trial of, 109–17.

UNITED STATES: BAILOUT OF FINANCIAL MARKETS IN, 20–21; financial sector profits in, 13, 138 n.16; housing market in, 74–76, 149 n.27; regulation of financial markets in, 13, 18, 22, 29, 136 n.12, 140 n.3.

United States Steel Corporation, 31–32.

Use value, 35–38, 51, 63, 156 n.2.

U.S. Supreme Court, 158 n.20.

U.S. Treasury bonds, 31.

VALUE, 35–41, 43–45; as exchange value, 27, 37–41, 156 n.2; fetishizing of, 51–61; as hedging value, 27–28, 36–41, 44–45, 60, 150 n.14; of labor power, 64–84; Marx's analysis of, 35–41, 43–46, 50, 63, 156 n.2, 163 n.47; as use value, 35–38, 51, 63. *See also* Securitized capitalist relations.
Value at risk (VaR), 151 n.23.
Vampire analogy, 124–25, 178 n.36.
Vampire squid analogy, 9, 23, 27, 125.
Volcker, Paul, 92–93.

WALL STREET, 9–10; annual earnings on, 173 n.4; Museum of American Finance on, 31–32; New York Stock Exchange on, 32–33; power of institutions of, 20–21, 141 n.14; quantitative finance experts of, 9, 17–23, 140 n.2, 142–43 n.15, 143 n.17. *See also* Goldman Sachs; Subprime mortgage crisis of 2008.
Washington, George, 31.
Wealth of Nations (Smith), 149 n.6.
Weather derivatives, 25–26, 62.
Weber, Max, 120.

Welfare states, 88–95, 167 n.25; demise of, 93–95, 145–46 n.24, 166 n.18; social contract of, 88–93, 96.
White, Harry Dexter, 91.
Williams, John Burr, 41, 151 n.18.
Wolf of Wall Street , The (Scorsese), 64.
Working classes: commodification of labor and wage relation of, 26–29, 34–35, 63–65, 68, 82–84, 86, 90, 103; declining wages of, 95; dismantling of organized labor and disempowerment of, 15, 22–23, 95; easy credit for, 23, 95–100; individualized risk of, 93–95, 167 n.25, 167 n.30, 172 n.56; as insecure neoliberal subjects, 26–27, 78, 87–89, 96–97, 106–107, 169 nn.37–38; Marx's history of emergence of, 85–88, 96–97, 105, 159 n.37, 169 n.37; social contract of, 88–93, 96; as subprime borrowers, 97–100, 121–24. *See also* Probable man.
World Bank, 91.

ZOMBIE CAPITALISM, 22–23, 27, 125–27, 143 n.17, 178 n.37.

ZONE BOOKS *NEAR FUTURES* SERIES
Edited by Wendy Brown and Michel Feher

The turn of the 1980s marked the beginning of a new era in the Euro-Atlantic world: Inspired by the work of neoliberal economists and legal scholars, the "conservative revolutionaries" who came to power during these pivotal years used their offices to undermine the thinking and dismantle the institutional framework upon which welfare capitalism had rested. In their view, the role of the government was not to protect vulnerable segments of the population from the potential violence of market relations but, instead, to shelter the allegedly fragile mechanisms of the market from stifling rules and the disabling influence of so-called "special interests" which ranged from organized labor to protectors of the environment. They also believed that, once markets were properly shielded, their domain could be extended beyond the traditional borders of the private sector.

Eager to blunt the resistance raised by their agenda, neoliberal reformers initiated a series of deregulations, regarding capital flow and asset creation, that were meant to replace social protection and guaranteed employment with abundant and accessible credit—thereby endowing all economic agents with entrepreneurial ambitions and discipline. Yet, under the guise of diffusing the ethos of the self-reliant entrepreneur throughout the entire population, their reforms eventually enabled the speculative logic of financial markets to preside over the allocation of resources on a global scale. Thus, far from restoring thrift and frugality as the virtuous paths to personal independence and lasting profit, the reign of deregulated finance defined success as leverage, understood as the ability to invest with borrowed funds, and compelled the less fortunate to stake their livelihood on perennial indebtedness.

Much more than a mood swing, whereby the advocates of freer markets would temporarily prevail over the harbingers of a more protective State, the policies instigated under Ronald Reagan and Margaret Thatcher, and further refined by their "Third Way" successors, have successively transformed everything from corporate management to statecraft, household economics to personal relations. In the world shaped by these transformations—a world where the securitization of risks and liabilities greatly widens the realm of potentially appreciable assets—even the criteria according to which individuals are incited to evaluate themselves no longer match the civic, business, and family values respectively distinctive of political, economic, and cultural liberalism.

Along the way, the purchase of markets and "market solutions" has expanded to a range of domains hitherto associated with public services or common goods—from education to military intelligence to environmental stewardship. Simultaneously, the number and purview of democratically debatable issues has been drastically reduced by the sway of "good governance" and "best practices"—two notions originating in a corporate culture devoted to the creation of shareholder value but later co-opted by public officials whose main concern is the standing of the national debt in bondholders' eyes.

For a long time, many critics on the left hoped that the changes they were witnessing might be transient. As the unconstrained quest for short-term capital gain would bear its bitter fruits, the thinking went, gaping inequalities and the prospect of an environmental catastrophe would induce elected officials to change course or, if they failed to do so, expose them to a massive popular upheaval. However, neither the steady deterioration of labor conditions nor the increasingly alarming damages caused to the environment has acted as the anticipated wake up call. To the contrary, the aftermath of the Great Recession has demonstrated the remarkable resilience of a mode of government, disseminated across public and private institutions, that gives precedence to the gambles on tomorrow's presumptive profits over the mending of today's social woes and the prevention of after-tomorrow's ecological disaster.

Once filled with the hopes and apprehensions of radical change, the near future has been taken over by speculations on investors' tastes. As such, it mandates the sacrifice of the present and the deferral of any serious grappling with long-term sustainability. Yet, for those who wish to uncover alternative trajectories, the ultimate purpose of exposing the current dominance of speculators and the nefarious effects of their short-termism is not to forego the near future but to find ways of reclaiming it.

Reckoning with the epochal nature of the turn that capitalism has taken in the last three decades, the editors of *Near Futures* seek to assemble a series of books that will illuminate its manifold implications — with regard to the production of value and values, the missions or disorientations of social and political institutions, the yearnings, reasoning, and conduct expected of individuals. However, the purpose of this project is not only to take stock of what neoliberal reforms and the dictates of finance have wrought: insofar as every mode of government generates resistances specific to its premises and practices, *Near Futures* also purports to chart some of the new conflicts and forms of activism elicited by the advent of our brave new world.

Near Futures series design by Julie Fry
Typesetting by Meighan Gale
Printed and bound by Maple Press